A GUIDE TO EFFECTIVE PRAYER

The
MIGHTY
WARRIOR

THE MIGHTY WARRIOR
A Guide to Effective Prayer

by Elizabeth Alves

"The effective prayer of a righteous man
can accomplish much."
James 5:16

"Without God, we cannot.
Without us, God will not."
—St. Augustine

**CANOPY
PRESS**
Bulverde, Texas

THE MIGHTY WARRIOR
A Guide to Effective Prayer

By Elizabeth Alves

Unless otherwise indicated, Scripture quotations are from the New American Standard Bible, © 1960, 1962, 1963, 1968, 1971, 1972, 1973, 1975, 1977, by the Lockman Foundation, used by permission.

Intercessors International
P.O. Box 390
Bulverde, Texas 78163
(210) 438-2615

Dedicated to

*The glory of God, the Father,
His Son and the Holy Spirit*

and to

*Faithful intercessors throughout the
world who stand in the gap for His
leaders, continually building a hedge of
protection around them, that kings and
kingdoms might be changed for the glory
of God.*

ACKNOWLEDGMENTS

The task of writing increases in ease and enjoyment when God provides helpers to stand beside the writer to encourage, advise and assist. I have been especially blessed in all these ways and many more.

First of all, my husband, Floyd, provided prayer support and patiently advised, corrected and encouraged me when I thought it was an impossibility.

From the beginning, Carrie Hoffman, a very special friend, both challenged and inspired me to write this book. I would not have continued if it had not been for her encouragement and prayer support.

For more than six months, Quinett Sherrer worked almost full-time on researching the material. She literally built the foundation.

My friend, Ruthanne Garlock, and Linda Fletcher, my Administrative Assistant, worked many hours to complete the final editing.

Barbara Myers, for many years my Administrative Secretary, patiently typed and retyped the manuscript as it went through many transitions. What tenacity!

It was Chris Cooper, Resource Development Coordinator, who spent many hours working on the revision.

Joanna Virden immersed herself in Scripture to help compile the daily prayers and Maury Lloyd's expertise provided the logo and graphics.

The office staff, Ron Carl, Greg Carl and Cindy Divers united together to lend a helping hand wherever needed. What a blessing.

Russ Whitley and Tommi Femrite teamed together to encourage and advise in the revision.

Special thanks to my prayer partners—who are such a spiritual strength to me—who helped birth this book into reality through many hours of prayer. And to our partners in ministry whose love gifts made it all possible.

But most of all, I give thanks to the Lord Jesus Christ who allows us to know Him intimately through the wonderful gift of prayer.

THE MIGHTY WARRIOR

CONTENTS

FOREWORD

A great prayer movement began sweeping the world in 1970. It had been going on long before that in Korea, then God started bringing the rest of the Body of Christ on board. Pastors of all denominations in all parts of the U.S.A. are talking about prayer, teaching prayer, and praying more than any time in living memory. And the interest in prayer continues to increase. Many feel that we are now witnessing the precursor of the great revival, a worldwide outpouring of the Spirit of God on all flesh which will see vast multitudes turn to Jesus and glorify God.

I personally began to tune in to the prayer movement in 1987, making it a high agenda item for my research, writing, teaching and personal ministry. I'm rather embarrassed to admit that previous to 1987 I knew relatively little about prayer. As I began to collect a considerable amount of the available literature on prayer, one of the items I secured was *The Mighty Warrior*, at that time published in a preliminary edition. As I read *The Mighty Warrior*, I became very glad that Elizabeth Alves had been a long-standing participant in the prayer movement, and that she had decided to share what she had learned with those like me. This was just the book I needed. In a rare combination of thoroughness and conciseness, Beth Alves provided exactly the information I was looking for. I used it as an outline to teach some of my first lessons on prayer.

Later I found out that Beth Alves was an unusual person who had gained a widespread reputation as one of America's foremost prayer leaders. Even before I had met her personally, I knew that she had a delightful mix of both giftedness for intercession and much experience in praying and mentoring others for prayer ministries. I have now had the privilege of knowing Beth for some time, and I greatly admire her as a person of integrity and as a woman of God.

The Mighty Warrior is the right book at the right time. The demand for a basic guidebook on all the facets of prayer is escalating rapidly because of all the Christian people who are tuning in to what the Spirit is saying to the churches about prayer these days. God is calling out a vast army of His people to pray, and they are saying, "Show me how!" I have found no better training manual than this book. It explains what prayer is, what is does, what different kinds of prayer look like, how to hear from God as you pray, the essentials of spiritual warfare, and more.

Reading and applying the principles of *The Mighty Warrior* has all the potential to turn your church around and to impact your community decisively for the Kingdom of God.

—C. Peter Wagner
Fuller Theological Seminary
Pasadena, California

INTRODUCTION

This book is based upon a passage from Isaiah which affirms God's work through us, His pray-ers and His intercessors, in these last days before the Lord's return:

> On your walls, O Jerusalem, I have appointed watchmen; all day and all night they will never keep silent. You who remind the Lord, take no rest for yourselves; and give Him no rest until He establishes and makes Jerusalem a praise in the earth.
>
> *Isaiah 62:6,7*

Jerusalem and other ancient cities had regular guards or watchmen who were stationed on the city walls night and day to be on the lookout for danger. They were required to call to each other every few minutes—especially in times of danger—with the cry passing from one to another entirely around the city walls. Watchmen also had a station at the gate of a city and in the adjacent tower, as well as on hilltops overlooking terraced vineyards. A watchman held a responsible office requiring much vigilance and fidelity.

The word *watchman* comes from a Hebrew root meaning, "to hedge about (as with thorns); to guard, generally to protect and observe from a distance."

The modern counterpart to the Old Testament watchman is the intercessor. The city of Jerusalem is symbolic of the Church—the Body of Christ—over which the intercessors must watch and pray, until God establishes it "a praise in the earth." And just as in ancient times an enemy would seek to destroy the leaders of a city, then take the people captive, so today we see the enemy attacking the Church by attempting to destroy her spiritual leaders.

In the Jewish tradition, a *watch* was a three-hour period; eight such watches kept guards on a constant lookout over the city for its protection. In Gethsemane, Jesus asked the disciples to keep only one-third of a watch. "He came to the disciples and found them sleeping, and said to Peter, 'So, you could not keep watch with Me for one hour?'" *(Matthew 26:40)*. As a result, they were totally unprepared when the betrayer and the soldiers came to arrest Jesus.

A desire to pray and communicate with the Lord and to be able to hear His voice is something that is birthed within us. I have found over the years that most people hear the voice of the Lord, but just don't recognize it. This can cause frustration in prayer and intercession.

Like the disciples, I found myself asking, "Lord, teach me how to pray." The Lord honored that prayer by gifting me with a mentor, the late Vinita (Nonnie) Copeland. She taught me the simplicity of prayer with dynamic results. By spending hours in prayer with her, I found prayer was not a formula but a way of life. It is as important as daily bread. It was at her feet and through her example that I found my call to intercession, and later to the ministry that I now head, Intercessors International.

This ministry began in 1987 with the release of the first edition of the Prayer Manual and the recruitment of a group of intercessors who pledged to pray for missionaries, ministers, and spiritual leaders. It was a small but fruitful beginning. While the leaders began to feel the impact of committed prayer coverage, the intercessors increased their vision as they saw their prayers make a difference in the lives of those on the front lines of ministry.

THE MIGHTY WARRIOR is not a book of rules and formulas. It is a guideline to help enhance your prayer life and to give you a better understanding of the basics of prayer.

It is my prayer that as you read and study this book, you come into a greater knowledge of Jesus, His Word and His ways, as you learn to fellowship at His feet and become a Mighty Warrior through prayer.

—Elizabeth Alves
Intercessors International

I TRAVELED ON MY KNEES

Last night I took a journey to Israel across the seas, I
did not go by boat or plane, I traveled on my knees.
I saw so many people there with scars and wounds
within,
But God told me that I should go—there was oil to
pour from Him.
I replied, "Lord, I cannot go and work with such as
these,"
He answered quickly, "Yes you can, by traveling on
your knees."
He said, "You pray, I'll meet their need, you call and
I will hear,
Be concerned about the fate of those both far and
near."
And so I tried it, knelt in prayer, gave up some
hours of ease,
I felt the Lord right by my side while traveling on
my knees.
As I prayed on and saw them helped, and the badly
wounded healed,
I saw God's workers' strength renewed while
laboring on the field.
I said, "Yes, Lord, I have a job—my desire Thy will
to please,
I can go and heed Thy call by traveling on my
knees."

—Adapted from a poem
by Sandra Goodwin

PURPOSE
OF PRAYER

PURPOSE OF PRAYER

WHAT IS PRAYER AND WHY DO WE PRAY?

PRAYER IS THE RESPONSIBILITY OF EVERY CHRISTIAN. We are to obey God's Word, and He has told us to pray. The purpose of prayer is to determine God's will in a matter, and then to pray it into existence. It is a privilege and duty to be involved with God in the formative work of others' lives. "More things are wrought by prayer than this world dreams of," wrote Alfred Tennyson more than a hundred years ago—but it is still true today.

> First of all, then, I urge that entreaties and prayers, petitions and thanksgivings, be made on behalf of all men, for kings and all who are in authority, in order that we may lead a tranquil and quiet life in all godliness and dignity.
>
> *1 Timothy 2:1,2*

> Moreover, as for me, far be it from me that I should sin against the Lord by ceasing to pray for you; but I will instruct you in the good and right way.
>
> *1 Samuel 12:23*

> With all prayer and petition pray at all times in the Spirit, and with this in view, be on the alert with all perseverance and petition for all the saints.
>
> *Ephesians 6:18*

> Keep watching and praying, that you may not enter into temptation; the spirit is willing, but the flesh is weak.
>
> *Matthew 26:41*

> Pray without ceasing.
>
> *1 Thessalonians 5:17*

PRAYER IS A PRIORITY AND A LIFESTYLE. Prayer had priority in Jesus' life over physical rest, over social life and even over food. Prayer was the primary communication link between Jesus and His Father; the same is true for us.

> And after He had sent the multitudes away, He went up to the mountain by Himself to pray; and when it was evening, He was there alone.
>
> *Matthew 14:23*

> And it was at this time that He went off to the mountain to pray, and He spent the whole night in prayer to God.
>
> *Luke 6:12*

PRAYER IS A MINISTRY UNTO THE LORD! You are called a priest unto Him. Ministry to God must come before ministry to people. Do not fail as God's child to minister to Him through praise and worship, and commune with Him through prayer and meditation.

This priestly duty is bestowed upon you because of the blood of Jesus. His blood has made you righteous so that you may enter into the Holy of Holies. Therefore, come boldly with confidence into His presence.

> But you are a chosen race, a royal priesthood, a holy nation, a people for God's own possession, that you may proclaim the excellencies of Him who has called you out of darkness into His marvelous light.
>
> *1 Peter 2:9*

> You also, as living stones, are being built up as a

spiritual house for a holy priesthood, to offer up
spiritual sacrifices acceptable to God   through
Jesus Christ.

1 Peter 2:5

...just as He chose us in Him before the
foundation of the world, that we should be holy
and blameless before Him.   In love He
predestined us to adoption as sons through Jesus
Christ to Himself...

Ephesians 1:4,5

The sacrifice of the wicked is an abomination to
the Lord, but the prayer of the upright is His
delight.

Proverbs 15:8

(Delight means to be pleased with; specifically
to satisfy a debt.)

(Also see *2 Corinthians 5:21* and *Hebrews 4:16.*)

PRAYER IS A UNIQUE CHANNEL OF
DIALOGUE BETWEEN YOU AND THE LORD.
It is spending time with Him because you love Him.
Your conversation will deepen into communion as
you share heart to heart with Him.   Even as He
made His ways known unto Moses and His acts to
the children of Israel, He can do the same for you.
The Lord speaks today through the Holy Spirit.

Thus the Lord used to speak to Moses face to
face, just as a man speaks to his friend. When
Moses returned to the camp, his servant Joshua,
the son of Nun, a young man, would not depart
from the tent. Then Moses said to the Lord,
"See, Thou dost say to me, 'Bring up this
people!' But Thou Thyself hast not let me
know whom Thou wilt send with me.
Moreover, Thou has said, 'I have known you by
name, and you have also found favor in My

sight.' Now therefore, I pray Thee, if I have found favor in Thy sight, let me know Thy ways, that I may know Thee, so that I may find favor in Thy sight. Consider too, that this nation is Thy people." And He said, "My presence shall go with you, and will give you rest."

Exodus 33:11-14
(Also see verses 15-23.)

PRAYER CAUSES YOUR SPIRITUAL EYES TO BE OPENED SO YOU CAN SEE INTO THE SPIRITUAL REALM. Keenness in the Spirit realm comes as you discipline yourself in prayer, praise, fasting and renewing your mind through God's Word. Ask the Lord to reveal spiritual reality to you like Elisha did when he asked God to open his servant's eyes and allow him to see the chariots of protection.

So he answered, "Do not fear, for those who are with us are more than those who are with them." Then Elisha prayed and said, "O Lord, I pray open his eyes that he may see." And the Lord opened the servant's eyes, and he saw; and behold, the mountain was full of horses and chariots of fire all around Elisha.

2 Kings 6:16,17

And Jesus said, "Who is the one who touched me?" And while they were all denying it, Peter said, "Master, the multitudes are crowding and pressing upon You." But Jesus said, "Someone did touch Me, for I was aware that power had gone out of Me."

Luke 8:45,46

JESUS, OUR GREAT INTERCESSOR, GIVES YOU A PERFECT EXAMPLE BY HIS LIFE OF PRAYER. Prayer is one of the most Christ-like examples you can follow in your Christian walk. It is an unselfish work and usually is not seen or appreciated by others; they only experience the results. You are not seeking to be seen by men, but to stand in the presence and pleasure of the Lord.

> Christ Jesus is He who died, yes, rather who was raised, who is at the right hand of God, who also intercedes for us.
>
> *Romans 8:34b*

> And in the early morning, while it was still dark, He arose and went out and departed to a lonely place, and was praying there.
>
> *Mark 1:35*

> Hence, also, He is able to save forever those who draw near to God through Him, since He always lives to make intercession for them.
>
> *Hebrews 7:25*

> (Jesus Himself would often slip away to the wilderness to pray. See *Luke 5:16*.)

PRAYER IS A LOVE RESPONSE TO OTHER PEOPLE'S BURDENS. You have the privilege of interceding on behalf of others. You can feel the heart of the Father and experience His heart hurting for His children through the Holy Spirit.

Many times we read of Paul's prayers and love response to others in his writings:

> I thank my God in all my remembrance of you, always offering prayer with joy in my every prayer for you all...For it is only right for me to feel this way about you all, because I have you in my heart.
>
> *Philippians 1:3,4,7*

> For this reason I too, having heard of the faith in the Lord Jesus which exists among you, and your love for all the saints, do not cease giving thanks for you, while making mention of you in my prayers.
>
> *Ephesians 1:15,16*

> Do nothing from selfishness or empty conceit,
> but with humility of mind let each of you regard
> one another as more important than himself; do
> not merely look out for your own personal
> interests, but also for the interests of others.
>
> *Philippians 2:3,4*

PRAYER IS GOD'S OWN WORD ALIVE IN YOUR MOUTH. Praying God's Word brings results and answers. You must speak forth the Word in faith, not in vain repetitions or by way of a formula. The Word of God must be quickened by the Holy Spirit so you may speak forth with anointing.

God desires you to come to Him with FAITH, believing. He assures you He will work in cooperation with you.

> And without faith it is impossible to please
> Him, for he who comes to God must believe
> that He is, and that He is a rewarder of those
> who seek Him.
>
> *Hebrews 11:6*

> So shall My word be which goes forth from My
> mouth; it shall not return to Me empty, without
> accomplishing what I desire, and without
> succeeding in the matter for which I have sent
> it.
>
> *Isaiah 55:11*

PRAYER BEARS FRUIT FOR THE KINGDOM AND PLEASES GOD. When you pray and communicate with God, He speaks to you and will give you direction, wisdom, knowledge, strength, and protection.

> For this reason also, since the day we heard of
> it, we have not ceased to pray for you and to
> ask that you may be filled with the knowledge
> of His will in all spiritual wisdom and

understanding, so that you may walk in a manner worthy of the Lord, to please Him in all respects, bearing fruit in every good work and increasing in the knowledge of God; strengthened with all power, according to His glorious might, for the attaining of all steadfastness and patience.

Colossians 1:9-11

I waited patiently for the Lord; and He inclined to me, and heard my cry. He brought me up out of the pit of destruction, out of the miry clay; and He set my feet upon a rock making my footsteps firm.

Psalm 40:1,2

If you abide in Me, and My words abide in you, ask whatever you wish, and it shall be done for you. By this is My Father glorified, that you bear much fruit, and so prove to be My disciples.

John 15:7,8

PRAYER MAKES A WAY SOVEREIGNLY FOR GOD TO ACT ON EARTH. Jesus said to pray, "Thy will be done on earth as it is in heaven" *(Matthew 6:10).* He also says, "Truly I say to you, whatever you shall bind on earth shall have been bound in heaven; and whatever you loose on earth shall have been loosed in heaven" *(Matthew 18:18).* The obvious inference is that God has limited some of His activities in the earth and will respond only to the prayers of His children.

Heaven waits for those of us on earth to pray for things to happen. E. Stanley Jones once said, "We align ourselves with the purpose and power of God, and He is able to do things through us that He could not do otherwise." God seeks for a man, an intercessor, to plead for His perfect will to be done on earth as it is in heaven.

> Put Me in remembrance; let us argue our case together, state your cause, that you may be proved right.
>
> *Isaiah 43:26*

> Then the Lord said to me, "You have seen well, for I am watching over My word to perform it."
>
> *Jeremiah 1:12*

PRAYER CAN CAUSE GOD TO RELENT FOR HIS GLORY. Many times the fate of the world is not in the hands of governors or kings, but in the hands of mighty intercessors. You, too, can influence society as Abraham and Daniel did in the Old Testament. It is exciting to realize that your prayers not only affect those you are praying for, but could actually mold national or international events.

> Then Moses entreated the Lord his God, and said, "O Lord, why doth Thine anger burn against Thy people whom Thou hast brought out from the land of Egypt with great power and with a mighty hand? Why should the Egyptians speak, saying, 'With evil intent he brought them out to kill them in the mountains and to destroy them from the face of the earth'? Turn from Thy burning anger and change Thy mind about doing harm to Thy people. Remember Abraham, Isaac, and Israel, Thy servants to whom Thou didst swear by Thyself, and didst say to them, 'I will multiply your descendants as the stars of the heavens, and all this land of which I have spoken I will give to your descendants, and they shall inherit it forever.'" So the Lord changed His mind about the harm which He said He would do to His people.
>
> *Exodus 32:11-14*

(Also see *Genesis 18:17-30; Numbers 14:11-23; 1 Samuel 7:8-13; 2 Kings 20:1-11; Daniel 9:2,3.*)

THROUGH PRAYER YOU RECEIVE REVELATION AND THE MIND OF GOD. God will reveal to you through the Holy Spirit what He desires you to pray for, and will pinpoint a problem area in someone's life or in a situation. He allows you to see as He sees, but the intercessor must guard carefully the secrets God reveals during prayer. He must be obedient to share only when the Lord directs. Seek His clear guidance on the proper follow-up of His revelation.

> At that time Jesus answered and said, "I praise Thee, O Father, Lord of heaven and earth, that Thou didst hide these things from the wise and intelligent and didst reveal them to babes. Yes, Father, for thus it was well-pleasing in Thy sight."
>
> *Matthew 11:25,26*

> All things have been handed over to Me by My Father, and no one knows who the Son is except the Father, and who the Father is except the Son, and anyone to whom the Son wills to reveal Him.
>
> *Luke 10:22*

> Let us, therefore, as many as are perfect, have this attitude; and if in anything you have a different attitude, God will reveal that also to you.
>
> *Philippians 3:15*

THROUGH PRAYER, THE KINGDOM OF GOD BECOMES REAL THROUGH MIRACLES OF GOD OPERATING IN YOUR LIFE. You will see the manifested power of God confirm your spiritual walk.

> But the news about Him was spreading even farther, and great multitudes were gathering to hear Him and to be healed of their sicknesses.

But He Himself would often slip away to the wilderness and pray.
Luke 5:15,16

And these signs will accompany those who have believed: in My name they will cast out demons, they will speak with new tongues; they will pick up serpents, and if they drink any deadly poison, it shall not hurt them; they will lay hands on the sick, and they will recover. And they went out and preached everywhere, while the Lord worked with them, and confirmed the word by the signs that followed.
Mark 16:17,18,20

YOU ARE CALLED TO DO SPIRITUAL WARFARE THROUGH PRAYER OVER SATAN'S STRONGHOLDS UNTIL YOU WIN!

Jesus Himself had to battle Satan through prayer for His ministry and in other situations. We find this clearly illustrated in His wilderness temptation. He experienced spiritual warfare and WON before He ever went out into public ministry. You, too, must win before you can fully function in what God has called you to do. The success of Jesus' life, and yours, is dependent on winning...winning in prayer. (See *Joshua 1:3,11,15*.)

Then the devil left Him; and behold, angels came and began to minister to Him.
Matthew 4:11

But no one can enter the strong man's house and plunder his property unless he first binds the strong man, and then he will plunder his house.
Mark 3:27

Daniel also had to battle Satan in prayer.

Then he said to me, "Do not be afraid, Daniel, for from the first day that you set your heart on understanding this and on humbling yourself before your God, your words were heard, and I have come in response to your words. But the prince of the kingdom of Persia (Satan's emissary) was withstanding me for twenty-one days; then behold, Michael, one of the chief princes, came to help me, for I had been left there with the kings of Persia."

Daniel 10:12,13

PRAYER IS AN INVITATION FOR YOU TO REST IN HIM. God invites you to give Him your problems, cares, concerns, worries.

Casting all your anxiety upon Him, because He cares for you.

1 Peter 5:7

Do not be anxious for your life...look at the birds of the air...your heavenly Father feeds them. Are you not worth much more than they?

Matthew 6:25,26

Cast your burden upon the Lord, and He will sustain you; He will never allow the righteous to be shaken.

Psalm 55:22

Be anxious for nothing, but in everything by prayer and supplication with thanksgiving let your requests be made known to God. And the peace of God, which surpasses all comprehension, shall guard your hearts and your minds in Christ Jesus.

Philippians 4:6,7

HOW LONG DO I PRAY?

It is clear from the account of Jesus and His disciples at Gethsemane that Jesus felt asking His followers to pray with Him for one hour was a perfectly legitimate request. Yet, at the time when He needed and desired their support, they disappointed Him. Surely it must still disappoint our Lord when His followers put sleep and other activities above a desire to pray and spend time with Him. One pastor has said, "When you come to the place where you can tarry with the Lord one hour, something supernatural happens. You begin to understand the character and purposes of God, and to experience the anointing of the power of God as never before."

If making a commitment to pray one hour a day seems too difficult for you, begin by praying fifteen minutes a day, then strive to increase your prayer time.

As you pray, a basic question may come to mind: "How long should I spend on each person or subject?" Here are some suggestions:

> Pray until an answer is received and you literally see the fulfillment of it come to pass.

> or

> Pray until you have the assurance from the Lord that it is accomplished in the spiritual realm. How? By exhausting your efforts or until you have peace. Then accept it by faith. When you do your part in intercession, you must

trust God's timing. He is never late, though it seems to His children that He passes up many opportunities to be early!

Once you have prayed through your own daily strategy, praise is always in order. Give Him praise and thanksgiving for the victory gained.

If an answer is long in coming, be tenacious and follow the example of the widow:

> Now He was telling them a parable to show that at all times they ought to pray and not to lose heart, saying, "There was in a certain city a judge who did not fear God, and did not respect man. And there was a widow in the city, and she kept coming to him, saying, 'Give me legal protection from my opponent.' And for awhile he was unwilling; but afterward he said to himself, 'Even though I do not fear God nor respect man, yet because this widow bothers me, I will give her legal protection, lest by continually coming she wear me out.'" And the Lord said, "Hear what the unrighteous judge said; now shall not God bring about justice for His elect, who cry to Him day and night, and will He delay long over them? I tell you that He will bring about justice for them speedily. However, when the Son of Man comes, will He find faith on the earth?"
> *Luke 18:1-8*

The word "bothers" (verse 5) used in the New American Standard translation comes from a Greek word meaning, "to beat the breast in grief; to lament or mourn; to give trouble to." The idea is to pray persistently and tenaciously.

When a response is delayed, continue to hold fast

in prayer, like the widow in *Luke 18*. Do not cast away your confidence as you wait on the Lord; if you grow weary and give up, the fruit of your prayer can be aborted.

> And I say to you, ask, and it shall be given to you; seek, and you shall find; knock, and it shall be opened to you. For everyone who asks, receives; and he who seeks, finds; and to him who knocks, it shall be opened.
>
> *Luke 11:9,10*

Therefore, keep on asking, keep on seeking, keep on knocking—KEEP ON!

Is all this repeated asking vain repetitions or lack of faith? NO, this kind of repetition is not wrong as long as it is spoken in faith. Prayer is only vain repetition when you speak empty words without faith behind them or if you ask with a wrong motivation. (See *James 4:3*.)

Jesus gives us a good example of being tenacious and asking with the right motive. During His Gethsemane ordeal it is written that Jesus specifically prayed, "My Father, if it is possible, let this cup pass from Me; yet not as I will, but as Thou wilt" (*Matthew 26:39*).

Jesus made this same request three times.

> And again He went away and prayed, saying the same words.
>
> *Mark 14:39*

> And he left them again, and went away and prayed a third time, saying the same thing once more.
>
> *Matthew 26:44*

WHEN DO I PRAY?

As for me, I shall call upon God; and the Lord will save me. Evening and morning and at noon, I will complain and murmur, and He will hear my voice.

Psalm 55:16,17

When the Holy Spirit calls you to pray, let nothing stand in your way. Obey the urgency of the Spirit to pray immediately when you feel an inner witness or urge to pray for someone or something! Your immediate response can change the direction of a person's life, or a situation, for the purpose of God's glory and their good.

You can accomplish far more through prayer than through your works and deeds. You are meeting with God Himself, asking divine intervention. Procrastination can be your greatest enemy, so use your time wisely, being careful not to waste it.

When you pray is up to you. The most important thing is that you set aside time each day to meet with the Lord.

Study the following scriptures to see what the Word advises, then ask God at what time He wants you to intercede.

Examples and Scriptures

Morning

Psalm 5:3
Psalm 88:13
Mark 1:35
Acts 2:1-4,15 (This points out that the Holy
                Spirit fell at 9 a.m.)

Noon
Psalm 55:17

Evening

Matthew 14:23	Luke 6:12
Mark 6:47	Acts 16:25

Continuously

1 Samuel 7:8	Romans 1:9,10
1 Samuel 12:23	Ephesians 6:18
Nehemiah 1:6	Colossians 1:9
Psalm 72:15	Colossians 4:2
Luke 2:37	1 Thessalonians 3:10
Luke 6:12	1 Thessalonians 5:17
Acts 10:2	1 Timothy 5:5

Keep in mind that Jesus prayed early in the mornings and often all night!

WHERE DO I PRAY?

There are many examples of places to pray in the Bible. The place is not as important as following the instructions of Jesus:

> And when you pray, you are not to be as the hypocrites; for they love to stand and pray in the synagogues and on the street corners, in order to be seen by men. Truly I say to you, they have their reward in full. But you, when you pray, go into your inner room, and when you have shut the door, pray to your Father who is in secret, and your Father who sees in secret will repay you.
>
> *Matthew 6:5,6*

Secret means "concealed from public view or from general knowledge," or "operating in a hidden or confidential manner."

The inner room, or inner chamber, was usually

an upper story built on the roof of a house. It was strategically located on the city walls facing or overlooking the city gate. The chamber could be used as a watchtower to spot the enemy or observe a victory parade. It was also a high place for an altar and a place of prayer.

When you participate in inner chamber prayer, the Word states that the Father will reward you openly. However, you do not have to be in an inner room to be in communion with the Lord. You can be in a park, on a train, driving on the highway, etc., with others all around you when the Holy Spirit nudges you to pray. While driving in traffic, you can practice "intersection intercession."

While you are advised to set aside a certain time to be alone for prayer, be alert because the Holy Spirit may quicken to you a special concern that needs immediate prayer, regardless of where you are.

There are many places mentioned in the Bible as places people prayed, but here are a few listed from the New Testament:

Upper room............................... *Acts 1:13,14*
House .... *Acts 10:30; 12:5-17*
By a river .... *Acts 16:13*
On a beach .... *Acts 21:5*
Wilderness .... *Luke 5:16*
Lonely place .... *Mark 1:35; Luke 4:42*
Mountains................... *Matthew 14:23; Mark 6:46;*
Luke 5:16; 6:12; 9:28;
John 6:15
Alone .... *Matthew 6:6; 26:39;*
Mark 6:46; 14:32-42;
Luke 6:12; 9:18; 22:41

IN WHAT POSITIONS DO I PRAY?

Just as there are various places to pray, there are also a variety of postures for prayer. But the leading of the Holy Spirit as you yield to Him is more important than the position you are in.

Here are some examples listed in the Bible:

SITTING

1 Chronicles 17:16-27

KNEELING

*1 Kings 8:54; Ezra 9:5;
Luke 22:41; Acts 9:40*

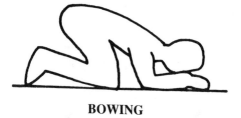

BOWING

*Exodus 34:8; Nehemiah 8:6;
Psalm 72:11*

STANDING

Nehemiah 9:5;
Mark 11:25;
Luke 18:13

WITH UPLIFTED HANDS

2 Chronicles 6:12,13;
Psalm 63:4;
1 Timothy 2:8

WALKING

2 Kings 4:35

PROSTRATE

Joshua 7:6; Ezra 10:1;
Matthew 26:39; Mark 14:35

TYPES OF PRAYER

TYPES OF PRAYER

PRAISE AND THANKSGIVING

The first step in prayer is to remember you are entering the very presence of God. You talk and share your heart with Him because you love Him.

The Word tells us that PRAISE and THANKSGIVING are important keys that allow you to enter into His presence:

> Enter His gates with thanksgiving, And His courts with praise. Give thanks to Him; bless His name.
>
> *Psalm 100:4*

As you enter into praise, meditate on the provision the Lord has made for you through the blood of Jesus. His blood allows you to walk today in the new covenant *(Hebrews 10:19; 12:24).*

PRAISE GOD FOR WHO HE IS!

The source of PRAISE is the Holy Spirit activating your spirit to express approval and adoration of God's greatness. Develop the habit of PRAISE during your prayer time.

> O Lord, open my lips, that my mouth may declare Thy praise.
>
> *Psalm 51:15*

> Seven times a day I praise Thee, because of Thy righteous ordinances.
>
> *Psalm 119:164*

As you begin to PRAISE and extol the Lord, your spirit helps you to rise to a higher level in the understanding of who He is. Your soul is also strengthened in the process of praise because you have the knowing that there is nothing too difficult for Him *(Jeremiah 32:17)*.

THANK HIM FOR WHAT HE HAS DONE AND WHAT HE WILL CONTINUE TO DO.

Thanksgiving awakens your love toward God as you acknowledge you are His child. Thank Him that He gives you every good and perfect gift *(James 1:17)*. In your prayer time, respond with joy to His benefits showered on you as His heir.

> In all your ways acknowledge Him, and He will make your paths straight.
>
> *Proverbs 3:6*

> What shall I render to the Lord for all His benefits toward me? To Thee I shall offer a sacrifice of thanksgiving, and call upon the name of the Lord.
>
> *Psalm 116:12,17*

PRAISE WORKSHEET

With these thoughts, begin to PRAISE and THANK Him. Express your love and adoration for Him. Acknowledge His attributes through His different names. (See "Names of God.")

Here are expressions of praise in seven Hebrew words in the Old Testament:

* TOWDAH: Sacrifice of thanksgiving

or praise; to render thanksgiving or praise. (See *Psalms 42:4; 100:4.*)

* YADAH: To throw, thrust or cast away from, hands outward, to throw hands into the air. (See *Psalms 67:3; 107:8,15,21,31.*)

* BARAK: To bless, to give thanks and praise to God because He has given out of His abundance; bless as an act of adoration, to kneel. (See *Psalms 31:21; 63:4; 95:6.*)

* HALAL: To make a show or boast, to be clamorously foolish, to go about in a raging or raving way, to dance, to celebrate. (See *Psalms 56:4; 150:1,2.*)

* ZAMAR: To celebrate with instruments, to praise the Lord skillfully on an instrument, to touch strings with the fingers. (See *Psalms 21:13; 33:2; 98:4.*)

* TEHILLAH: Imperative summons to praise Jehovah. A psalm or a hymn, by choirs, with dancing and expressive speaking; festal jubilation. (See *Psalms 22:3,25; 33:1; 35:28.*)

* SHABACH: Praise, comment, soothe, still; adoration towards the power, glory and sanctity of the Lord. Praise God for His mighty acts and deeds. To triumph in a loud voice. (See *Psalms 63:3,4; 117:1; 147:12.*)

A joyful way to start a prayer time is to choose a Psalm or several verses from the Bible and go through each expression of praise. This will energize your spirit. Psalms 145-150 are especially good because they exalt God for His goodness, love, power, holiness, wisdom, greatness, glory, and majesty.

Start with *Psalm 145:1-7*:

> I will extol Thee, my God, O King; and I will bless Thy name forever and ever. Every day I will bless Thee, and I will praise Thy name forever and ever. Great is the Lord, and highly to be praised; and His greatness is unsearchable. One generation shall praise Thy works to another, and shall declare Thy mighty acts. On the glorious splendor of Thy majesty, and on Thy wonderful works, I will meditate. And men shall speak of the power of Thine awesome acts; and I will tell of Thy greatness...and shall shout joyfully of Thy righteousness.

THANKSGIVING WORKSHEET

Here is an adaptation of *Psalm 136*. It is great for motivating you in THANKSGIVING towards the Lord.

I give thanks to You, Lord, for (list a person). Your lovingkindness is everlasting. I give thanks to You, Lord, who has given (list a material blessing). Your lovingkindness is everlasting. I give thanks to You, Lord, who has given (list a spiritual blessing). Your lovingkindness is everlasting. I give thanks to You, Lord, who has heard my prayer for (list something you are asking for). Your lovingkindness is everlasting. I give thanks to You, Lord, who has answered my prayer for (you fill in). Your lovingkindness is everlasting. I give thanks to You, Lord, who has (you fill in). Your lovingkindness is everlasting. I give thanks to You, Lord, who has (you fill in). Your lovingkindness is everlasting. I give thanks to You, Lord, who has (you fill in). Your lovingkindness is everlasting. I give thanks to You, Lord, who has (you fill in). Your lovingkindness is everlasting.

CONFESSION AND FORGIVENESS

CONFESSION and FORGIVENESS are the appropriate responses to the holiness of God. You must set your will to have a pure, undivided heart and a right attitude toward every person, including the Lord God. This is a prerequisite to effective intercession!

You can confess your sins for hours on end, but CONFESSION is not complete unless it is coupled with forgiveness.

CONFESSION means "to acknowledge or disclose something damaging or inconvenient to one's self; to acknowledge or admit something."

FORGIVENESS means "to excuse a fault or offense; to pardon; to relinquish anger, resentment, or bitterness against a person; to absolve from payment of."

So you see, one is not complete without the other. After CONFESSION and FORGIVENESS, you must go one step further and receive the provisions God has granted you through His Word, such as healing, peace, and prosperity. Many people confess and forgive, but make the mistake of not receiving God's special promises because they feel unworthy. This is a false concept. God's promises are a special gift to you.

Learn to be a good receiver. Receiving means to acquire or take something offered or given.

Receiving requires action on your part. Quote God's promises aloud and accept them by faith, not relying on your feelings or emotions.

Through this process of CONFESSION and FORGIVENESS you are restored to sonship. Praise the Lord for His blood which ransoms you and pays your debt.

Now let us discuss CONFESSION and FORGIVENESS separately:

CONFESSION

Consider the following scripture:

> Behold, the Lord's hand is not so short that it cannot save; neither is His ear so dull that it cannot hear. But your iniquities have made a separation between you and your God, and your sins have hidden His face from you, so that He does not hear.
>
> *Isaiah 59:1,2*

As this verse explains, iniquities can cause your prayers not to be heard. Confession must take place before you enter into intercession or petition so that your prayers are pleasing to His ears.

You cannot be purified in your own power and strength. God provides the Holy Spirit to shine on your sins so you can confess them. During your prayer time, pause and ask the Holy Spirit if there is any matter which needs to be confessed. At this time respond to Him with your answer.

> Examine me, O Lord, and try me; test my mind and my heart. For Thy lovingkindness is before my eyes, and I have walked in Thy truth.
>
> *Psalm 26:2,3*

Once an area of darkness has been brought to the light of God's Word and repented of, in no way should you look back. When a sin has been dealt with, know that the power of the blood of Jesus covers it and the Lord remembers it no more. Do not try to bring up past sins that have already been covered by the blood of Jesus. The Lord has buried them in the depths of the sea and they are forgotten.

> If we confess our sins, He is faithful and righteous to forgive us our sins, and to cleanse us from all unrighteousness.
>
> *1 John 1:9*

> It was for freedom that Christ set us free; therefore keep standing firm and do not be subject again to a yoke of slavery.
>
> *Galatians 5:1*

> If we say that we fellowship with Him and yet walk in the darkness, we lie and do not practice the truth; but if we walk in the light as He Himself is in the light, we have fellowship with one another, and the blood of Jesus His Son cleanses us from all sin.
>
> *1 John 1:6,7*

> He will again have compassion on us; He will tread our iniquities underfoot. Yes, Thou wilt cast all their sins into the depths of the sea.
>
> *Micah 7:19*

Be aware that one of Satan's tactics is to bring you into condemnation or guilt by bringing to your mind past sins. Through introspection, he desires that you keep your mind centered on yourself and away from prayer, praise, and pulling down his strongholds. The battleground is your mind.

> For the weapons of our warfare are not of the

> flesh, but divinely powerful for the destruction of fortresses. We are destroying speculations and every lofty thing raised up against the knowledge of God, and we are taking every thought captive to the obedience of Christ, and we are ready to punish all disobedience, whenever your obedience is complete.
>
> *2 Corinthians 10:4-6*

Let God's peace guard your heart and mind daily through Jesus Christ to prevent this struggle. If our heart condemns us, then we cannot ask in faith. We are double-minded and cannot pray in confidence (*James 1:6*). Peace of mind comes by continual prayer.

> Be anxious for nothing, but in everything by prayer and supplication with thanksgiving let your requests be made known to God. And the peace of God, which surpasses all comprehension, shall guard your hearts and your minds in Christ Jesus.
>
> *Philippians 4:6,7*

When confessing your sins, know that you do not have to have an emotional experience to be forgiven. First ask, then accept by faith in God's Word that He will do exactly as He says...that He is faithful and just to forgive you (*1 John 1:9 KJV*).

FORGIVENESS

Unforgiveness breaks your full communication with the Lord. It desensitizes you to spiritual things.

When you ask FORGIVENESS for yourself and those who have sinned against you, you will be set free and able to walk in right relationship to God and man. FORGIVENESS also frees the other person or changes circumstances causing the problem. It allows the Holy Spirit to do His job and convict of sin, righteousness and judgment.

If you are having a problem forgiving someone, determine to obey God's Word and not be guided by your feelings. Do not let pride keep you from having a right relationship with God. Lay down your hurts, self-righteous attitude and hostilities. Forgive that person who has wronged you, no matter how unjust the offense may be. You will then experience a release in your spirit, and your feelings will begin to come into line. Your fellowship with the Lord is restored.

There are three areas of unforgiveness:

1. *Not forgiving people* who have hurt or offended you.

2. *Not forgiving God* because in your perception He did not intervene on your behalf in the way you wanted Him to.

3. *Not forgiving yourself* for situations you have experienced or participated in causing you hurt, guilt, condemnation, worry, frustration, etc.

God's Word says, "For if you forgive men for their transgressions, your heavenly Father will also forgive you. But if you do not forgive men, then your Father will not forgive your transgressions" *(Matthew 6:14,15)*. Many times you will find it easier to forgive others or to forgive God, than to forgive yourself. But total forgiveness is essential to your effective praying.

It is good to make a decision every morning that you will walk in forgiveness that day. Do not wait until you get into a confrontation and then try to forgive the person who has wronged you. Choose to forgive others as God has forgiven you, and do it immediately at the time of the offense, as Jesus did (*Luke 23:34*).

FORGIVENESS in itself is not enough; you must also REPENT. To repent is to feel such regret or remorse that you turn away from your thoughts or actions and release others from any bondage you or they hold. Unless this is done, you will never be free. Forgiveness and repentance go hand in hand. (*Proverbs 28:13; Matthew 3:6,8*)

Many times people are weak or in ill health emotionally and physically because of unforgiveness and unrepentance. This does not mean all suffering from ailments is because of unforgiveness. But forgiveness and repentance can release the healing power of God in you and in others.

FORGIVENESS, like confession, does not have to be an emotional experience. It is simply an ACT OF YOUR WILL responding to the Word of God by the prompting of the Holy Spirit.

Once you have forgiven others or God or yourself, know that the Lord is faithful and righteous to forgive you of your sin and cleanse you from all unrighteousness (*1 John 1:9*). Do not depend on your own understanding; trust the Lord, for His Word is true.

If your mind's attention is repeatedly drawn in a negative way to a person you have chosen to forgive, you must take authority over your thoughts. Command your mind, in Jesus' name, to dwell on thoughts that are true, honorable, right, pure, lovely, excellent and worthy of praise. (*Philippians 4:8,9*) Order the enemy to be silent, and stop listening to your old memory circuits. Change direction by believing what God's Word says. It is helpful to quote scripture verses aloud until you have the victory. You can also begin to thank the Lord for the positive qualities He has placed in that person and in the situation, and pray God's blessing upon these positive areas.

CONFESSION AND FORGIVENESS WORKSHEET

Are you ready to be clean? Take time to allow the Holy Spirit to search your heart before God; ask Him to show you your own heart. Don't search your own heart with your natural mind; you must perceive your own heart by the Holy Spirit. As you accept the Lord's cleansing and forgiveness, ask Him to refill you with the Holy Spirit.

Here are scripture-based prayers of CONFESSION and FORGIVENESS that might help you when you pray:

PRAYER OF CONFESSION

Father, I thank You for the blood of Jesus that cleanses me from all my sin. I come before You in the name of Jesus and ask to be restored to a right relationship with You and my brothers and sisters in Christ.

Father, Your Word says that if I confess my sin You are faithful and just to forgive me and cleanse me from all unrighteousness. I come into Your presence to confess my sin of _____, knowing that I can draw near with a true heart in full assurance of faith, having my heart sprinkled from an evil conscience and my body washed with the pure water of Your Word.

Be gracious to me, Father. Blot out my transgression of _____. Wash me thoroughly from this iniquity and cleanse me from my sin. It is only against You, Lord, that I have sinned and done what is evil in Your sight. I ask Your forgiveness.

I now rejoice, not that I was made sorrowful, but that I was made sorrowful to the point of repentance. My repentance, according to Your will, leads me to eternal life in You. I receive Your abundant life where I was dead in sin. For the law of the Spirit of life in Christ Jesus has made me free from the law of sin and death. And whom the Son sets free shall be free indeed; blotting out the handwriting of ordinances that were against me, which was contrary to me, You took it out of the way by taking it to Your cross. I choose now to walk under this new covenant of liberty in Your Spirit life.

Father, I thank You that You have blotted out my sin(s), and as far as the east is from the west is how far You have removed them from me. I declare that this day my sin will be remembered no more, and if Satan brings it up again, he will have to deal with You.

(1 John 1:7,9; 5:6-9; Hebrews 10:22; Psalms 51:1-4; 103:12; Colossians 2:14; Romans 4:7; 8:2; John 5:24; 8:32; 2 Corinthians 3:6; 7:9-19; Ezekiel 18:11; 33:16)

PRAYER OF FORGIVENESS

Father, I come before Your throne with a heavy heart because _(person or persons)_ has offended me and I have unforgiveness. I know unforgiveness is contrary to Your Word. Because of this, I have been tormented in my mind and emotions. This has created a binding tie between me and _____.

Therefore, I ask, Father, that You forgive my sins of _____, and I also forgive _(person or persons)_ as You have forgiven me. I repent and let go of all bitterness, wrath, anger, clamor, slander, animosity and malice. I receive my forgiveness in Jesus' name and by His precious blood.

Thank You, Father, for setting _____ and me free from all mental and emotional torment. I will not give the devil an opportunity. I will guard my mouth and let no unwholesome word come forth concerning _(person or persons)_. I will speak words of life, power, health and healing. I will not grieve the Holy Spirit. I will be kind, tender-hearted, forgiving other people as You have forgiven me. I will not return evil for evil, or insult for insult, but I will speak words of blessing upon _____.

I will walk in a manner worthy of You, Lord. I will determine to please You in all my actions and thoughts. I will bear fruit in every good work because I am a doer of Your Word and not a hearer only.

In Jesus' name, I command freedom to my body, soul, spirit, family, and finances, because I am no longer under the curse of the law but have received my liberty.

I ask that the Holy Spirit rule in my life, bearing fruit to please You. Today I put off my old nature and put on Your love, joy, peace, patience, kindness, goodness, faithfulness, gentleness and self-control.

By a choice of my will, I make a fresh commitment to You, Lord, that I will live in peace with the saints and with my friends, co-workers, neighbors and family.

(Isaiah 59:1,2; Mark 11:25; Matthew 6:12,14,15; 18:21-35; 1 Peter 2:1,2; 1 John 1:6,7; Ephesians

4:25-32; 1 Peter 3:8-12; Colossians 1:10; 3:10; James 1:22,25; Galatians 3:13,14; 5:22,23; Romans 12:10,16-18; Philippians 2:2)

INTERCESSION

Jesus, your great high priest, provided the example of how to intercede when He was on earth, and assured you that He continues to intercede even now in heaven (*Hebrews 7:25*). Therefore, when you intercede, you are following His example.

The Bible tells you to intercede, and explains why:

> First of all then, I urge that entreaties and prayers, petitions and thanksgivings, be made on behalf of all men, for kings and all who are in authority, in order that we may lead a tranquil and quiet life in all godliness and dignity. This is good and acceptable in the sight of God our Savior.
>
> *1 Timothy 2:1-3*

THE INITIATIVE FOR INTERCESSION COMES FROM GOD! As an intercessor, you must be sensitive and responsive to the direction of prayer the Holy Spirit places on your heart. When Abraham was interceding for the city of Sodom, God said, "Shall I hide from Abraham what I am about to do?" (*Genesis 18:17*). Abraham was trying to save the whole city, not just Lot and his family. God communed with Abraham as a friend.

Intercession has been described as a love response to the prompting of the Holy Spirit for an urgent need. It can be a very simple cry to the Lord for someone you love. All His children are called to participate in intercession.

"Bear one another's burdens, and thus fulfill the law of Christ" (*Galatians 6:2*). God is pleased when you are a burden-bearer for others, coming in intercession on their behalf.

Daniel chapter 10 records an instance when Daniel received a message from God concerning a great conflict between the angelic hosts. The Hebrew word translated "message" is sometimes translated "burden." Often when God gives you a message or a word, there is a heaviness or a burden placed upon you to pray that word into action. Sometimes the directive will be to pray the Word of God. At other times you may be led to do warfare against the enemy forces. Sometimes intercession may cause an anguish of heart, or a wrestling within your spirit.

You must be available to receive a prayer message or prayer burden from God. It is a holy trust when the Lord reveals His secrets to you in this way; do not take it lightly. When you feel the power of the Holy Spirit moving within your heart, be obedient to cry out to God on behalf of a spiritual leader, nation or an individual as the Spirit brings names and places to your mind. Effective prayer requires availability, sensitivity and obedience.

Another admonition to intercede is:

> If My people who are called by My name humble themselves and pray, and seek My face and turn from their wicked ways, then I will hear from heaven, will forgive their sin, and will heal their land. Now My eyes shall be open and My ears attentive to the prayer offered in this place.
>
> *2 Chronicles 7:14,15*

How do you know what to pray for? The Scriptures give you guidelines, and the Holy Spirit brings to you the most urgent requests.

> Make me know Thy ways, O Lord; teach me
> Thy paths, lead me in Thy truth and teach me,
> for Thou art the God of my salvation; for Thee I
> wait all the day.
>
> *Psalm 25:4,5*

> The secret of the Lord is for those who fear
> Him, and He will make them know His
> covenant.
>
> *Psalm 25:14*

One way to begin is to ask:

"Lord, what do you want me to pray for this person today?"

"What is on Your heart?"

"What is the most pressing need?"

"Show me how to intercede."

You may ask, "How will I know if the Holy Spirit is calling me to pray?" The Holy Spirit will show you by words, messages, or thoughts that stir your spirit. Sometimes these will totally surprise you. (See "Hearing the Voice of God.")

Here are some examples to identify a call to prayer:

* The Holy Spirit brings to mind a face, a name, a family, a church, a situation, a nation or a scene.

* God places a practical need upon your heart; perhaps one you have observed or heard expressed in everyday conversation. (Examples: a friend calls requesting prayer, news media alerts you to a current event, you can't get someone off your mind, etc.)

* Something you witness—such as a car accident, a passing ambulance, a person in obvious need, someone being abused, or a crime taking place—prompts you to pray.

Remember, intercession generally is begun and ended by God. After He gives you a subject or topic to pray about, you should pray until you feel He wants you to move on to the next area. It can be prayer for spiritual and for physical blessings; it can be spiritual warfare on someone's behalf. If you do not have a special impression or particular direction, let the Holy Spirit guide you until you feel a release.

Do not be surprised if occasionally you experience something unusual or unexpected, such as laughter, groans, weeping, or travailing sounds. Paul said, "My little children, of whom I travail in birth again until Christ is formed in you" (*Galatians 4:19 KJV*).

Do not be afraid if you experience unusual emotions, nor be concerned if you do not pray in this manner. The emphasis is not on a travailing type of prayer, but it sometimes accompanies deep intercession. Many times you may pray in a very authoritative manner over the principalities and powers of the evil, unseen world.

When the burden for prayer is lifted, you may experience other emotions, such as peace, joy accompanied with laughter, or tears. Regardless of your feelings, know that your petitions have touched the Father's heart.

PETITION

PETITION is humbly making a formal request or supplication (to beg or beseech) to one in authority.

When petitioning, you are asking the Lord for a specific grant or benefit, earnestly entreating Him for grace, mercy and favor towards a particular need.

How do you petition the Lord?

* You are to come to the Lord in childlike faith with your specific requests, knowing how much He desires to give good gifts to His children.

> If you then, being evil, know how to give good gifts to your children, how much more shall your Father who is in heaven give what is good to those who ask Him!
>
> *Matthew 7:11*

> Truly I say to you, whoever does not receive the kingdom of God like a child shall not enter it at all.
>
> *Luke 18:17*

> You ask and do not receive, because you ask with wrong motives, so that you may spend it on your pleasures.
>
> *James 4:3*

What are the conditions for asking?

* Make sure your petition is properly motivated and that it will glorify the Lord *(John 14:13; James 4:2,3)*. Do not ask out of sheer selfishness.

* Ask in faith without doubting. Asking plus believing will assure you of receiving. *(Matthew 21:21,22; Mark 11:23; Hebrews 3:12; James 1:6)*

* Ask in accordance with His will; His Word

must be inside your heart *(John 15:7; Romans 10:8-10; 1 John 3:18-22; 5:14,15)*.

* Abide in the true vine—Jesus. Abiding is a two-way commitment. You must hear, believe and do His Word; then the Father, Son and Holy Spirit will make their abode with you. *(John 14:23; 15:1-10)*

* Bear good fruit; it must also be lasting. His disciples prove to be good fruit bearers. *(Matthew 7:15-27; 15:13; Luke 3:8,9; 8:14,15; John 15:2,16; Jude 12,13)*

* Ask in the name of Jesus. He has given you the authority to use His name. His name has power on earth and in heaven and hell. Everything has to bow to His name. *(John 14:13; 16:23b-24; Philippians 2:9,10)*

What should I ask for?

Whatsoever things you desire... *Mark 11:24*
(Also see *John 14:14; Philippians 4:6.*)

Through the Holy Spirit the Lord will place a need or desire upon your heart. When this is done, agree with the Holy Spirit, yield your will to His and begin to make your requests known to the Lord.

As you pray and petition the Lord, He will birth a vision (mental impression) within your heart. This vision will always be in line with God's Word. It must not be otherwise! (See "Hearing the Voice of God.")

PETITIONS MUST BE SPECIFIC REQUESTS. Hannah, who wanted a baby with all her heart, petitioned God for a child. Yet she asked specifically for a son, making an unselfish vow to give him to the service of God. The Lord heard, granted her request, and she conceived and bore a son; then she was obedient to her vow. Hannah had had a need for a long time, but when she expressed that need aloud, petitioning the Lord specifically, with a pure heart, she received exactly what she asked *(1 Samuel 1 and 2)*.

Some other examples of petition are:

*   Jacob prayed for safety *(Genesis 32:9-12)*.

*   King Hezekiah asked God to spare his life *(2 Kings 20:1-11)*.

*   Abraham's servant prayed for success in his task of finding a wife for Isaac *(Genesis 24:12-14)*.

*   The blind man cried out to Jesus to regain his sight *(Mark 10:51)*.

God wants you to petition Him—to ask, to seek, to knock. For it is promised to you that if you ask, you will receive *(Matthew 7:7,8)*.

> And this is the confidence which we have before Him, that, if we ask anything according to His will, He hears us. And if we know that He hears us in whatever we ask, we know that we have the requests (petitions) which we have asked from Him.
>
> *1 John 5:14,15*

It is the Lord's pleasure to answer prayer. It glorifies Him *(John 14:13)*. But He wants you to do your part—to ask, to petition, be specific in prayer.

WHY DO PRAYERS GO UNANSWERED?

One of the frequent questions relating to prayer is, "Why did my prayer go unanswered?" Quite often that means, "Why wasn't my prayer answered the way I wanted it to be?" Or you may ask, "I know God can, but why hasn't He?"

We do not have all the answers on why prayers go unanswered, but the good news is we have some of the answers based on the Word of God. In this section we are going to concentrate on ten of the reasons. Often a negative statement can result in a positive answer, which is the method being used here.

* **NOT FELLOWSHIPING WITH GOD.** To fellowship with God is a call according to *1 Corinthians 1:9*. Fellowship means to have companionship, partnership, communion, to simply spend time with. A call means a summons, a request or an invitation. Jesus is a prime example on going to the mountain to pray all night, especially when major decisions had to be made *(Luke 6:12,13)*.

* **NOT PRAYING TO THE FATHER IN JESUS' NAME.** Jesus instructed His disciples on how to pray, and it is believed when Jesus said to do something a certain way, that is the way it should be, even today. Prayer is to be directed to the Father in Jesus' name *(John 15:16)*. This is a simple truth but not one that all Christians are following.

* **NOT ASKING, OR ASKING WITH WRONG MOTIVES**. Some people believe God is too busy to hear their little prayers. He says whatever you ask He hears. God wants more than your grocery list. He wants to dine with you. These truths are summed up in *James 4:2,3* and *Revelation 3:20*.

* **NOT ASKING ACCORDING TO GOD'S WILL**. God's will is learned by reading and hearing the Word of God, and spending time with Him. Salvation, for example, is explicit in God's Word. Men of God in the Bible knew His will when they prayed. Moses in *Exodus 32:11-14* is a good example. Also read *1 John 5:14,15*.

* **NOT HAVING GOD'S WORD IN YOU.** Jesus said in *John 15:7*, "If you abide in Me, and My words abide in you, ask what you desire, and it shall be done for you." The Bible on cassette tape is excellent also, even playing all night alongside your bed.

* **DOUBT AND UNBELIEF**. *James 1:5-8* tells you to ask of God in faith and without doubting for your request to be fulfilled. Jesus instructed His followers to believe for what they prayed and they would receive. Elijah the prophet, a man with a nature like ours, won great victories when he prayed *(1 Kings 18)*, then ran from one woman when doubt set in *(1 Kings 19)*.

* **LOSING HEART OR GIVING UP**. Many prayers are not answered affirmatively because someone loses heart or gives up.

This is best expressed in *Luke 18:1 (AMP)* when Jesus says that we ought always to pray and not to turn coward—faint, lose heart, give up. In the verses which follow in that chapter, the widow received because she kept asking.

* **NOT BEING IN AGREEMENT.** Jesus spoke on agreement in *Matthew 18:19*, "Again I say to you that if two of you agree on earth concerning anything they ask, it will be done for them by My Father in heaven." Marriage partners' agreement is the strongest on earth. Strife and contention are contrary to agreement and will hinder prayers.

* **UNFORGIVENESS.** One of the strongest statements by Jesus follows what is commonly called The Lord's Prayer. In *Matthew 6:14,15* He says, "For if you forgive men their trespasses, your heavenly Father will also forgive you. But if you do not forgive men their trespasses, neither will your Father forgive your trespasses." And did Jesus mean 490 times in *Matthew 18:21,22*? When there is consistent forgiveness, you wipe the slate clean and begin again at the count of one. God will not remember your sins when forgiveness is asked *(Isaiah 43:25)*.

* **NOT GIVING TITHES AND OFFERINGS.** Tithing was in the Old Testament, and can be found in the New Testament, plus the early believers were willing to give all *(Acts 2:44-47* and *4:32-37)*. Jesus had much to say about giving and the blessings thereof. "Do we give off the gross or the net?" is a common question. The answer is simple: Do you want a gross or a net blessing?

In conclusion, here are more reasons why prayers go unanswered, which if they apply, you may want to study further:

* DISOBEDIENCE
  (Deuteronomy 1:42-45; Isaiah 1:19,20; Hebrews 4:6)

* PREJUDICE AND HATE
  (Proverbs 26:24-28; 1 John 2:9-12; 3:15-22)

* UNREPENTED SIN
  (Psalms 19:12,13; 66:18; Isaiah 59:1,2)

* OVERINDULGENCE OR NOT CARING FOR YOUR BODY (GOD'S TEMPLE)
  (Proverbs 23:1-8; Luke 21:34; 1 Corinthians 3:16)

* TOUCHING GOD'S ANOINTED
  (1 Samuel 26:5-11; Psalm 105:15)

* FEAR
  (Psalm 56:4,11; Proverbs 29:25; 1 John 4:18)

* NOT EXAMINING YOURSELF BEFORE COMMUNION
  (1 Corinthians 11:27-31)

* DESPISING GOD'S WORD
  (Proverbs 28:9)

* INDIFFERENCE
  (Proverbs 1:24-28)

* NEGLECT OF MERCY
  (Proverbs 21:13)

* NOT HONORING ONE ANOTHER
  (Deuteronomy 5:16; 1 Peter 3:7)

* SETTING UP IDOLS
  (Anything you worship above God)
  (Deuteronomy 7:25-26; Joshua 7; Ezekiel 14:3)

* SPEAKING EVIL OF BRETHREN
  (Galatians 5:26; James 4:11; 5:9)

HEARING
FROM GOD

HEARING FROM GOD

HEARING THE VOICE OF GOD

The key to hearing the voice of God can be found in the scripture, "Draw near to God and He will draw near to you" *(James 4:8)*. He wants to speak to you personally, and you must individually hear His voice *(John 10:3-5)*. Drawing near to the Lord opens the door for Him to fellowship and communicate with you. It is His desire to teach you *(Psalm 32:8)*, lead you into the truth and show you things to come *(John 16:13-15)*.

The Lord speaks to you through the person of the Holy Spirit *(Ezekiel 36:27; John 14:16-17)*. Jesus calls Him a Counselor. The word counselor comes from the Greek word parakletos, and it literally means, "one called alongside to help." It also means comforter, strengthener, helper, advisor, advocate, intercessor, ally and friend. You need not be afraid to trust the voice of the Holy Spirit, remembering that He never moves outside of the character of the Lord and always is in harmony with the Word of God. He is your friend who is called to walk beside and communicate with you. His is not a silent friendship *(Psalms 28:7; 37:3; John 12:49; 14:26)*.

God wants to instruct you and give answers to your questions *(Psalms 21:2; 119:169)*. You cannot depend on another person to hear for you. Hearing the Lord's voice should be a normal, everyday occurrence to those willing to spend time with Him. You do this through studying God's Word, meditating upon and memorizing Scripture. *(Joshua 1:8; Psalm 119:11,16)*. Then when you hear His voice, you will know it because it is in agreement with the

Word of God. The more you know His Word, the more you will understand His character and His ways *(Exodus 33:13; Psalms 25:4; 103:7)*.

One way to know whether you are hearing the Holy Spirit is to use this test: Does the voice gently lead you in a direction, or is it commanding and harsh? God's voice gently guides and encourages, giving you hope *(Psalm 18:35; Isaiah 40:11; James 3:17)*. GOD LEADS, SATAN DRIVES *(John 10:4)*. God convicts, Satan condemns and brings guilt *(Psalm 8:1,2)*. God woos, Satan tugs hard. When God speaks, He does not use fear to motivate. If fear overcomes you, it is the enemy speaking, not God *(2 Timothy 1:7)*.

Proverbs 4:20,21 says:

> My son, give attention to my words; incline your ear to my sayings. Do not let them depart from your sight; keep them in the midst of your heart.

LISTENING—
A KEY PART OF INTERCESSION

Allow the Holy Spirit to reveal strongholds, special burdens, battle plans of the enemy, actions to take and prayer strategy. The Word commands us to keep on the alert; keep watching and waiting. Learn to identify His voice and be sensitive to respond quickly when He calls or answers.

SOMETIMES GOD IS SILENT. It can be frustrating when this happens, but keep waiting in faith and do not allow the enemy to cause you to succomb to unbelief *(Hebrews 4:11; 1 Peter 4:8,9)*. Focus on God's faithfulness and other positive attributes while you are waiting... *(Psalms 33:18 AMP; 36:5; 37:7,34; 143:1; Lamentations 3:25,26; Philippians 4:8).*

God's people needn't think that listening to Him is something difficult or only for the "spiritual" or "mature." Even in the early months of infancy a child learns to recognize the voice of the one who cares for him. It is the same with the Lord. The more time you spend with Him in total trust, just like a child, the more clearly you will recognize His voice. The more mature a child becomes, the better able he is to communicate. You need to make time to listen to the King of Kings, concentrating on what He is saying.

Jesus gave you His word that His sheep hear His voice. You are one of His sheep, and as long as you are part of the fold, you WILL hear His voice.

> My sheep hear My voice, and I know them, and they follow Me.
> *John 10:27*

> He who is of God hears the words of God.
> *John 8:47*

HOW DOES GOD SPEAK?

"God spoke to me" is probably one of the most misunderstood phrases among God's people; it can create an atmosphere of misunderstanding, confusion, hurt, rejection, jealousy, pride, etc. You may have run into someone who felt he had an edge on hearing from God, and that everyone must accept what he was saying.

If you are not familiar with the phrase, "God told me," or you do not understand how to hear God's voice, you might feel inferior, thinking God never speaks to you.

First, understand that God RARELY speaks in an audible voice. This can happen, but it is not the normal way in which God speaks to man. God is Spirit and communicates with you through His Holy Spirit within you.

> And I will ask the Father, and He will give you another Helper, that He may be with you forever, that is the Spirit of truth, whom the world cannot receive, because it does not behold Him or know Him, but you know Him because He abides with you, and will be in you. And in that day you shall know that I am in My Father, and you in Me, and I in you.

> If anyone loves Me, he will keep My word; and My Father will love him, and We will come to him, and make Our abode in him (you). But the Helper, the Holy Spirit, whom the Father will send in My name, He will teach you all things and bring to your remembrance all that I have said to you.

> *John 14:16,17,23,24,26*

If God does not speak audibly, how does He speak? He speaks to you through the Holy Spirit in the theater of your mind and through spiritual hearing—in the same way you use your natural mind and hearing.

You do not think in words, you think in pictures. Picture a friend saying to you, "You should have seen Tom (your best friend) on the street corner yesterday with his little girl. They were sharing about Jesus, and his daughter sang 'Jesus Loves Me' in such a special way." As you were being told, you could see Tom and his little girl sharing and singing. You could picture it in the theater of your mind and hear it with your inner ear because you know them both so well.

Another example: Suppose you'd just become engaged and wanted to tell your family. You would probably play this over and over again in the theater of your mind, seeing and hearing their reaction.

When God speaks to you, He speaks in the same way. As you begin to know Him through His Word, you will begin to recognize His character and His ways. It cannot be emphasized enough that the Holy Spirit NEVER speaks to you contrary to the Word.

HOW DO YOU EXAMINE A WORD WHICH YOU FEEL THE LORD HAS SPOKEN TO YOU?

First, you must go to the Word of God and see what He has to say about what you hear or see. How do you do this? You might want to start with a good Bible concordance and look up the words or word pictures as you receive them.

Let's take the example of my call to prayer. I heard, "Elizabeth, I have need of you." I began to meditate on each word the Lord spoke.

Obviously, I knew my own name, and the word "I" meant THE LORD, the I AM. "Have" means *now* or it could mean *in the future*. But what did Jesus have need of? Going to the concordance, I looked up "need." There I found that Jesus had need of only one thing—a donkey.

What then? I went to an encyclopedia and read about a donkey. The encyclopedia said it is a burden bearer and carries a weight many times greater than its size. It also relieves a person of a heavy weight or burden. And often it walks alongside.

Was the Lord calling me into intercession to help carry a burden for someone? (It was some time before this was confirmed and became a reality.)

GUIDELINES TO
HEARING THE VOICE OF GOD

* **BIND THE VOICE OF THE ENEMY**. When you pray, Satan will try to run interference. So before you start to pray, it is important to bind the voice of the enemy until you know and understand God's voice as well as that of your very best friend. Do this in the name of Jesus. Then trust the Holy Spirit. He will lead you and guide you into ALL truth. *(Matthew 16:19; John 14:26; 15:26,27; 16:13-15; James 4:7; 1 Peter 5:8,9)*

* **SUBMIT YOUR OWN WILL AND REASONING TO THE HOLY SPIRIT**. Many times your own will and reasoning get in the way of what the Spirit of the Lord wants to share with you or communicate to you. Trust in the Lord with all your heart and lean not on your own understanding. *(Psalm 119:104,125; Proverbs 3:5; 16:3; 1 Corinthians 2:14,16; James 4:7,8)*

* **TURN OFF YOUR OWN PROBLEMS**. Turning off your own problems isn't always easy but is necessary if you want true communication. Concentrating on your own problems forms a "static" that can interfere and bring confusion, causing a mixture of interpretation. *(Psalms 37:5; 42:5; 43:5; Proverbs 3:5; 14:30 AMP; Isaiah 26:3; Philippians 2:4; 4:6,7; 1 Peter 5:7)*

* **GIVE YOUR UNDIVIDED ATTENTION TO GOD'S WORD.** Focus your mind on what He is saying; hearing is passive, while listening is active. It will require mental effort and attention. Satan will fight you on this because the more revelation of God's Word, the more of a threat you will be to the kingdom of darkness. *(Psalm 37:7; Proverbs 4:4,20,23; 1 Corinthians 2:10-12; 2 Corinthians 10:5)*

* **LIMIT YOUR OWN TALKING.** After you have petitioned the Lord, take time to be still and wait upon Him. You do this in the same way you would carry on a conversation with a precious friend. *(Numbers 9:8; Psalms 18:28; 27:14; 31:24 AMP; 37:5; Song of Solomon 2:14)*

* **WRITE IT DOWN.** Listen to your inner thoughts and ideas. The Spirit of the Lord will speak to you through impressions or pictures in the theater of your mind. When this happens, write them down, because with time there is a tendency to forget. And the Lord might want to add more later. It will not be long before you will begin to see that what you have written fits into a pattern. As you continue to pray and see the answers to your prayers come to pass, certain pictures will take on a special meaning for you. *(Exodus 17:14; Psalms 16:7 AMP; 36:8b,9; 37:5; 77:6; Proverbs 9:10; 16:3,9; 1 Corinthians 2:9-16b)*

* **DON'T ARGUE MENTALLY.** Sometimes when the Spirit of the Lord speaks, you might

have a tendency to argue with yourself and say, "That's just me (or my imagination)." But as you check your written notes, God will give you confirmation from past times with Him, or He could be adding something for the future. *(Isaiah 46:10,11b; John 16:13; 1 Corinthians 2:16; 2 Corinthians 13:1b; Philippians 2:5)*

* **WAIT UPON THE LORD FOR THE INTERPRETATION**. Don't try to figure out impressions when you receive them. Wait upon the timing and wisdom of the Lord. *(Psalms 27:14; 37:7 AMP; Proverbs 2:6; 16:3; Daniel 2:22,23,28,30; John 10:4; Ephesians 1:17; Colossians 1:9)*

* **DON'T GET AHEAD OF (OR LAG BEHIND) THE HOLY SPIRIT**. Many times when the Lord shows or tells us something, we get so excited we run and share it; and the Spirit of the Lord isn't finished with us yet. Let Him develop the thoughts He gives you; wait until you know He is through. Don't try to make things happen. Proverbs 16:9 says, "The mind of man plans his way, but the Lord directs his paths and makes them sure." *(Jeremiah 10:23; 1 Corinthians 4:5a AMP; 2 Corinthians 4:6 AMP; 2 Peter 3:9a)*

* **BE TRUSTWORTHY**. The Lord will share with you just as you share with a friend. He expects the same from you that you expect out of the one with whom you share your personal confidences. The more He can trust you with deep and intimate things, the more He will entrust to you. *(Genesis 18:17-19;*

Numbers 12:7,8 AMP; Psalm 25:14; Isaiah 45:3)

* **THE HOLY SPIRIT SPEAKS THROUGH MUSIC.** There are times in the mornings when you wake up with a song on your heart, such as "Only Believe." Listen to the words; some time during the day it could be the very key you need to build your faith and lead you to victory. *(Exodus 15:1; 2 Chronicles 20:21,22; Psalms 32:7b; 40:3; 42:8; 77:6; 138:5; Ephesians 5:19; Colossians 3:16)*

* **PAY ATTENTION TO YOUR DREAMS.** The Lord often speaks in dreams and visions (word pictures). You will find that after awhile these will fit into a pattern, and certain pictures or circumstances will begin to mean something to you and will help you to interpret what you have dreamed. Not all dreams are of God; the ones that are will stand out to you and will leave a deeper impression on you. You will be able to remember them beyond just waking up in the morning. Remember to write them down; this is the only way you will be able to recall them when you need the details. Even if you don't understand the dream, write down what you think it means to you. (See "Journaling.") *(Job 33:14-16; Daniel 2:19-23; 4:18; 7:1,2, 7,13; 9:21,22; 10:14,21; Matthew 1:20; 2:13)*

* **DON'T BE AFRAID OF SILENCE.** Sometimes the Lord is silent. Don't get upset if you don't hear anything when you pray. Many times the Holy Spirit just wants to worship the Lord. When you have your heart

clean before Him, then there is nothing wrong. He just desires for you to come and bask in His presence because you love Him and want to be with Him. Just be still and know that He is God. *(Psalms 45:11; 46:10; 96:9; Song of Solomon 1:4; Isaiah 12:2,3; 30:15; 50:10)*

EXERCISE ON
HEARING THE VOICE OF GOD

Suppose someone said to you the word "man," then "woman," then "house." In the theater of your mind, you would **not** see the letters m-a-n, etc. What you would "see" is an impression of a man, woman or house.

Now let's change those same words to "my father," "my mother" and "my house." These words bring a totally different impression to your mind. Who do you love most in the whole world? Now the picture is entirely different.

Think back to a very memorable experience you and your favorite person shared. You do not see words, but rather an actual experience which has been indelibly imprinted upon your mind; you can "hear" and "see" what was said and done. You do not actually hear or see, but because this person is so special to you and the experience so profound, you can relive it again and again.

It is the same with the Lord. When you begin to spend time with Him and meditate on His Word, you, too, will see and hear Him and know Him even better than the person you love most in the whole world. This will naturally develop into an intimate, loving relationship between you and the Lord Jesus.

You have probably heard His voice many times,

and undoubtedly He has given you impressions or pictures which you did not realize were from Him.

FACETS OF THE HOLY SPIRIT

There are many facets to the personality of the Holy Spirit. He is a person, and just as you and I experience different emotions and express ourselves in diverse ways, so does the Holy Spirit. But He never moves outside of God's Word, or exalts or calls attention to the flesh.

When I was taught this in Bible school, it opened up my understanding in a whole new way to the personality of the Holy Spirit. It also helped me to understand the difference in people's responses during a worship service, prayer group or any other meeting.

Have you ever been in a service where the power of the Holy Spirit was so present and sweet, you felt like everyone should just be still and know that He is God? But the person next to you did not feel the same way. He was full of joy and excitement. He wanted to sing, clap or move about. And you wanted to say, "Shh, don't you know that the presence of the Lord is in this place?" At the same time he didn't understand why you were so somber. Perhaps both of you thought the other was missing the move of the Spirit. But really it was because the Holy Spirit was operating in a different facet through each of you.

Isn't this contrary to the character and harmony of the Lord? No! For example, men and women in the church do not all look alike, dress alike, talk alike or act alike. Neither will they act or look alike the same every day; they change day to day. It is the same with the Spirit of the Lord in you. As you yield to Him, the Holy Spirit will choose to move through you as He desires.

> Now there are varieties of gifts, but the same Spirit. And there are varieties of ministries, and the same Lord. And there are varieties of effects, but the same God who works all things in all persons.
>
> *1 Corinthians 12:4-6*

Let's look at some of the facets of the Holy Spirit.

* **CONVICTING OR PLEADING.** *John 16:8* says:

> And He (the Holy Spirit), when He comes, will convict the world concerning sin, and righteousness, and judgment; concerning sin, because they do not believe in Me...

Thus we see the Holy Spirit convicting or pleading with the unbeliever concerning sin, or righteousness or judgment. It is this facet that draws a person to Jesus. The Holy Spirit keeps His finger on what is wrong until it is settled. He often operates this way in church services.

Billy Graham reportedly told a group of ministers in Greensboro, North Carolina, when asked, "What is the secret to your ministry?" "If there is a secret to my ministry, it is not my secret, it is the secret of the Holy Spirit. There are two things that I rely on heavily—first is the convicting power of the Holy Spirit, and second, I say 'the Bible says.'"

Conviction can be a beautiful thing, but it can also be very painful. When the conviction of the Holy Spirit moves upon a person, many emotions are experienced. Don't interrupt when the Holy Spirit is dealing with someone; wait upon the timing of the Lord. Pray and lend yourself as an assistant to Him.

* **CLEANSING.** The censorial nature of the Holy Spirit is the holy cry (righteous indignation) within you that causes you to hate sin or to take authority over the devil. The Spirit of the Lord rises up within you and causes you to hate the sin that destroys the people of God. This is the facet of the Holy Spirit that Jesus operated in when He cleansed the temple.

> And they came to Jerusalem. And He entered the temple and began to cast out those who were buying and selling in the temple, and overturned the tables of the moneychangers and the seats of those who were selling doves; and He would not permit anyone to carry goods through the temple. And He began to teach and say to them, "Is it not written, 'My house shall be called a house of prayer for all the nations?' But you have made it a robber's den."
> *Mark 11:15-17*

Jesus was angry at the sin committed against the physical temple of God, not at the people. It is the same today, only now His children are the temple of the living God; one not made of stone. When the Lord desires to cleanse His temples (man) today, He moves through the cleansing power of the Holy Spirit.

Paul tells us in *Ephesians 4:26-28* "..to be angry and yet do not sin; do not let the sun go down on your anger and do not give the devil an opportunity." When the Holy Spirit moves through you in such a way, you will experience God's anger through righteous indignation, and yet not sin against the Lord. This type of anger does not give place to Satan but has an exact opposite effect.

A well-known Bible teacher describes it in this way: "It is the Holy cry of the inner man by the Holy Spirit whereby the Spirit of God and the spirit of man in union cry out against that that's immoral, sinful, unjust, and destructive to God's kingdom and to the body, soul and spirit of man."

This facet of the Holy Spirit not only moves in righteous indignation against the sinful nature of others but also against that which is in you as well. It can be painful when the Spirit of the Lord begins to deal with your own nature in those things not pleasing to Him. As you allow His Spirit to drive out that which is unholy and unrighteous within you, you, too, will experience His cleansing power and this facet of His personality.

* **COMMUNION.** This facet of the Holy Spirit desires a time of communion and fellowship with you. Communion is the exchanging of ideas, opinions, thoughts or feelings. Communion interchanges with the word communicate.

It is the desire of the Lord for you to come

into His presence: He wants to share with you what is in His heart, and to hear what is on yours. In *John 17*, Jesus prays what is known as the High Priestly prayer. He prays to the Father for us to have the communion and fellowship with each other that They shared.

> I do not ask in behalf of these alone, but for those also who believe in Me through their word; that they may be one, even as Thou, Father, art in Me, and I in Thee...
> *John 17:20,21*

There are times when the Lord just wants to commune with you. He does this through many avenues, such as prayer, praise, worship, meditation and the study of God's Word.

The more you commune with the Lord, the more you will know Him and the more sensitive you will be to the other facets of the personality of the Holy Spirit.

* **COMPASSIONATE**. Compassion is a facet of the Lord that carries with it an inner emotion. In the Greek it literally means to have the bowels yearn...a yearning deep within the intestine. This is more than just a sympathetic concern, it creates an identity deep within that brings about the miraculous.

Every place in scripture that states Jesus was "filled with compassion" always brings with it a demonstration of the power of God for miracles. Jesus had compassion for the hungry and fed them all; He healed the blind, raised the dead, cast out demons, and cleansed the leper. Jesus was always touched by the Spirit of Compassion when He saw His people like sheep without a shepherd. *(Matthew 9:36; 14:14; 15:32; 20:34; Mark 1:41; 6:34; 8:2 and Luke 7:13)*

* **COUNSELING.** Jesus said it was advantageous that He go away and that He send a Counselor (Helper) to lead you and guide you into all truth. The Holy Spirit will not speak on His own authority, but whatever He hears, He will speak *(John 16)*. The Holy Spirit will teach and instruct through you.

A counselor not only gives advice, but exchanges opinions and ideas with you, helping you to reach a decision or set a direction. He is one called alongside to help.

In this facet, the Holy Spirit counsels you and speaks through you to help you counsel others. Have you ever been to lunch with someone who had a problem or need? You opened your mouth, and out came wisdom that even you marveled at. You were such a help to that person, you decided to meet the following week and talk again. But the next week the same wisdom and counsel were not there. What happened? The power of the Holy Spirit was present the first time, but the next week He did not come in the same way.

> But the Comforter (Counselor, Helper, Intercessor, Advocate, Strengthener, Standby), the Holy Spirit, Whom the Father will send in My name [in My place, to represent Me and act on My behalf], He will teach you all things.

> And He will cause you to recall—will remind
> you of, bring to your remembrance—
> everything I have told you.
>
> *John 14:26 AMP*

* **COMMANDING**. This is the preemptory facet of the Lord. His command terminates all debate or action. Webster's dictionary says, "...implies authority, power to control, and to require obedience." In the Greek it means to appoint or place appropriately, to appoint over and to put in charge.

Jesus was in a boat with His disciples, and a storm began to rage. His disciples became afraid and woke Jesus up because they thought they were perishing. Jesus commanded the storm to cease.

> And they (his disciples) came to Him and
> woke Him up, saying, "Master, Master, we
> are perishing!" And being aroused, He
> rebuked the wind and the surging waves, and
> they stopped, and it became calm. And He
> said to them, "Where is your faith?" And
> they were amazed, saying to one another,
> "Who then is this, that He commands even
> the winds and the water and they obey Him?"
>
> *Luke 8:24,25*

When you issue a command in the power of the Spirit of the Lord, you have the authority. You don't have to ask for it or demand it, it is yours by virtue of the Spirit of God. You cannot issue a command and expect results unless the Spirit of the Lord so directs. Prayer is an important part of knowing the will of God. When Paul fasted, the Lord gave the instructions.

There are many places in the Word where the Spirit of the Lord spoke a command and others obeyed, both in the spirit world and in the natural. Jesus commanded the spirits to leave, while Paul commanded the people not to leave the ship when it appeared to be sinking.

* **CONQUERING.** This facet of the Holy Spirit is the overcoming power of the Lord, that which causes you to be victorious. It is also the joy, triumph and exultation that comes forth when you know a victory has been won.

This is what the Lord gave David when he overcame Goliath. He knew who he was in the Lord, and he went forth to conquer without fear or doubt. *(1 Samuel 17)*

The joy of conquering was felt when Moses, Miriam, and the children of Israel sang the song of deliverance when they overcame the Egyptians. *(Exodus 15)*

There are many examples in the Word of God of the conquering facet of the Holy Spirit. And this we know, we are MORE THAN CONQUERORS IN HIM.

* **CONCERT.** When the Lord is moving in this facet, He moves through a melody within your heart. The dictionary describes a concert as: "An agreement of two or more in a design or plan; union formed by mutual communication of opinions and views; harmony."

In this facet the Lord will bring comfort, joy, peace, direction, guidance, etc. Songs have ministered comfort and victory in times of grief, such as the song, "It is well with my soul." It might come in the form of a chorus, song, poetry or melody you are familiar with, or it could come "hot off the press" from the Lord. You will see this facet work in harmony with all the other facets of the Spirit in a special way.

Now you will be able to appreciate the different responses you observe in a church service, meeting, etc. It's exciting to watch the Spirit of the Lord move differently in and through one another. You follow the Lord's leading in your own heart and let Him move through each person as He wills.

PROVE ALL THINGS

It is important that you not only learn to hear the voice of the Lord but that you prove (test and examine) all things.

> But examine everything carefully, hold fast to that which is good.
> *1 Thessalonians 5:21*

When you hear the voice of the Lord, you cannot rely on your feelings and opinions. It must be in line with God's Word and His character. The Holy Spirit will never overrule what the Word of God has spoken and declared to be true.

Here are a few ways for you to prove or test what you receive, or what is being said to you by others.

In the beginning it will take time, but as you grow in Him it will become easier and you will become more efficient and sure as His Word and ways become real to you. This is by no means all inclusive but a simple guide to follow, and it may help keep you from error.

* **NEVER LOOK TO MAN, BUT TO JESUS.** Never look to man or seek words or confirmation from him. Many times God will use man to confirm what He has spoken, but it will come to you unsolicited. It will be given in a manner of humility, and the person giving it will not seek affirmation himself.

* **NEVER SET A TIME LIMIT.** God's time and your time are not the same. There are prophetic words in the Bible that have not yet been fulfilled, but because the Lord has spoken them, they will be. When you receive something from the Lord, it will be in His timing, so don't give up. *(1 Chronicles 17:11,12; Ecclesiastes 3:11; Isaiah 2:2; 46:10,11b; Acts 7:17; 11:28; Revelation 1:1)*

* **ALWAYS CONFIRM WITH THE WORD OF GOD ANYTHING YOU RECEIVE.** The Lord will never tell you anything outside the bounds of His word. Even if it is exactly what you are looking for and confirms what you thought the Lord said, if it does not agree with the Word of God, throw it away. It will only lead you into deception.

* **DON'T TAKE SCRIPTURES OUT OF CONTEXT.** Look at the total meaning to avoid hurting or deceiving yourself or others.

Many times people not only take scripture out of context, they use scripture in part to "confirm" what they want or make it fit their situation or circumstance. God does use scripture to confirm, but not out of context. You must learn to judge according to the whole of scripture. Every jot and tittle is important. *(2 Peter 1:20,21).*

* **WHAT IF THE WORD YOU RECEIVE IS IN LINE WITH THE SCRIPTURES BUT YOU DON'T UNDERSTAND IT OR HAVE A WITNESS TO IT?** Put it away, pray over it, and let the Spirit of the Lord bring it to pass. Remember, the Lord knows the future, and it might be exactly what you need to confirm a situation or just to let you know that you are exactly where the Lord wants you. Give it the test of time. This is one of the reasons it is important that you have it written down. Then you will not have confusion and doubt in the days that are ahead.

* **DON'T JUDGE ANOTHER'S WORD.** Only God knows the thoughts and intents of a man's heart. Many times you do not know a situation or understand the depth of what a person might be going through. What means one thing to you might mean something entirely different to the person to whom it is given. *(Proverbs 14:10; Romans 14:4; 1 Corinthians 2:11)*

* **NEVER LET WORDS OR PICTURES BRING YOU INTO CONFUSION OR FEAR.** If that happens, it is not of the Lord. God is

not a God of confusion nor does He produce or use fear tactics to control you. *(John 14:27; Romans 14:17; 1 Corinthians 14:33; 2 Corinthians 2:11; 2 Timothy 1:7 AMP)*

* **HAS GOD PLACED A CONDITION ON THE WORD HE GAVE YOU?** "I will do this...if you will do that...." Many times God will give us promises, but we must first fulfill His conditions. *(Proverbs 2:1-6; 4:4)*

JOURNALING

Journaling is keeping a written personal record of experiences, observations, etc., on a regular basis.

"It is written" is found repeatedly in the Word of God. God, Himself, wrote the Ten Commandments for man. The scribes' role was very valuable during Bible days for recording important events and for keeping track of earlier writings and genealogies.

WHEN DO YOU KEEP A JOURNAL? You keep it as the Lord gives you impressions, words or scriptures that come to you in your prayer time. This is not necessarily every day, but often.

WHY DO YOU KEEP ONE? It is difficult to trust to memory all the things you hear and receive. This can be especially difficult if you do not fully understand what the Lord is saying. Journaling isn't for God, it's for you.

The Lord may speak things to you that will actually come about days, months or years later. How many times have you said, "If I could just remember...," or "If I had only written it down...."

Keeping a journal increases your faith as you

come to realize that you really do hear from the Lord, especially when the things you have written down begin to come to pass.

HOW DO YOU KEEP A JOURNAL? There are many different ways. Your journal should ALWAYS include any impression, scripture or picture you receive in your prayer time while praying for a person or situation. You should record not only what you have seen and heard, but your own feelings and interpretation at the time. Then when God answers, it is good to go back and check your feelings or impressions with the outcome.

Be sure you record the date each time you make an entry.

Journals do not have to be expensive or fancy. Some find a loose-leaf or spiral notebook adequate, or a daily log book. Others prefer to purchase a journal from a stationery store, or use a computer. You might want to try several different ways before you find one that works best for you. It is not important what you use; what is important is that you record your times with the Lord.

You might like to separate your journal into subjects that relate to you, such as: family, church, business, friends, impressions, etc.

Are you praying for a particular friend or family member? Put his/her picture at the top of the page, with your prayer requests under it and the answers as they come.

I would recommend that you write out any scriptures you receive, especially if you're a new Christian. This makes for a quicker reference when you look back to what the Lord spoke to you, and it helps you to commit it to memory.

When you receive a picture in the theater of your mind, draw it out. It doesn't have to be fancy, just something to jog your memory when you look back over it. It is good to label what or who each person or item might mean. Many times when it comes to remembering details, time can be your enemy.

Keeping a journal can be one of the most rewarding things you do for yourself. If you will be dedicated for twenty-one days, you will find you have established a habit pattern, and it will become much easier each time. Like all things worthwhile, it will take discipline, but the rewards are phenomenal.

RESPONSE

It is important, after the Holy Spirit has revealed the heart of the Lord to you, that you respond with an appropriate reply—an acknowledgment, a thank you, a shout of victory, or an action. Response to God sharpens your ability to hear. Enter freely into conversation with Him, and obey the directions He gives you.

During intercession try to pause and listen often. After each petition is prayed through, take time to bless the Lord for the work being accomplished for the Kingdom because of your prayers.

Always close your prayer in joy, gratitude, or praise, sealing the work of the Holy Spirit. The Lord's Prayer opens and closes with praise, giving you a good example to follow.

Don't become frustrated thinking you have to go through each procedure and response. It is the Holy Spirit that will lead you and guide you each step of the way.

PRAYER POINTERS

These guidelines are not intended to limit you in any way. Rather, we have endeavored to lay a basic foundation to start you in a direction of communicating and communing with the Lord. THE GREATEST NEED IS NOT THAT YOU ALWAYS HAVE GREAT REVELATION, OR PRAY BRILLIANT PRAYERS, BUT THAT YOU BE FAITHFUL TO THE CALL OF PRAYER. As you are obedient, The Lord's power will begin to flow. Even though you may not understand all the specific answers that come forth, you will see an awakening and strengthening of the Body of Christ *(Hebrews 11:13,39).*

* When you start to pray, begin with what you know are the obvious facts. Pray the Word and the precious promises of the Word given to us as His children.

* Always let the Holy Spirit be in charge. Remember you are just a soldier in the Army of God. Jesus is your "Commander in Chief." Let the Holy Spirit set the facet or the burden. Do not rely on your own insight *(Romans 8:26).*

* Pray with understanding in your native tongue, with singing and in the spirit *(1 Corinthians 14:15).*

* Pray in faith, expecting divine intervention. Pray in confidence. *(2 Corinthians 4:18; Hebrews 11:6; 1 John 5:14,15)*

* Take time to listen. It is an important part of communication and one of the keys to successful intercession.

* Keep praying until the answer comes. Before moving on, wait until the Holy Spirit assures you that the task is accomplished. *(Luke 11:5-10; 18:1-8)*

* Flexibility and speed of response are often critical to victory. The only obedience that impresses God is instant obedience.

* Meditate on the Word—renew your mind. Make sure all sin is under the blood of Jesus and that you are not harboring unforgiveness in your heart. *(Joshua 1:8; Proverbs 4:20-24; Hebrews 10:22; 1 John 1:7,9)*

SPIRITUAL WARFARE

SPIRITUAL WARFARE

IDENTIFY THE ENEMY

Dutch evangelist Corrie ten Boom said, "It's a poor soldier indeed who does not recognize the enemy." The key to victory in natural warfare, as well as in spiritual warfare, is to clearly identify the enemy, and to understand his character and his methods.

Who is the Christian's enemy? Satan and his host of fallen angels. Our opposition and struggle is against these unseen spiritual forces. (See *Isaiah 14:12-14; Ephesians 6:12; 2 Peter 2:4; Jude 6.*)

Webster's dictionary defines an enemy as a hostile force or power that has destructive effects. The Hebrew word often translated "enemy" in the Old Testament means "observer or one who is critically watching." The name Satan literally means "an adversary" or "one who accuses."

According to author C. S. Lewis, "Satan's cleverest trick is to convince the world that he does not exist." Few people, either Christian or non-Christian, have a clear concept of who Satan is and his place in the world. We succumb to our human reasoning in believing some *person* is our enemy—and act accordingly. Meanwhile, the real enemy, Satan, wreaks havoc in marriage relationships, families, churches, communities and nations.

Puritan pastor William Gurnall, in his book *The Christian in Complete Armour* (Volume One), illustrates our point in this way:

Spend your wrath on Satan, who is

your chief enemy. Men are only his puppets. They may be won to Christ's side and so become your friends at last. Anselm explains it in the following manner: "When the enemy comes riding up in battle, the valiant soldier is not angry with the horse, but with the horseman. He works to kill the rider so that he may possess the horse for his own use. Thus must we do with the wicked. We are not to bend our wrath against them, but against Satan who rides them and spurs them on. Let us pray fervently, as Christ did on the cross, that the devil will be dismounted and these miserable souls delivered from him."

Gurnall, pp. 140, 141

Satan was a perfect creature until he tried to exalt himself above God. His beauty filled him with pride—causing him to no longer be holy—and he wanted to receive worship that belonged only to God. Because Satan did not recognize the authority of God who made him, he was cast out of heaven, as recorded in the following passages:

> How you have fallen from heaven, O star of the morning, son of the dawn! You have been cut down to the earth, You who have weakened the nations!

> But you said in your heart, "I will ascend to heaven; I will raise my throne above the stars of God, And I will sit on the mount of assembly In the recesses of the north.

> I will ascend above the heights of the clouds;

I will make myself like the Most High."
Isaiah 14:12-14

You were the anointed cherub who covers, and I placed you there. You were on the holy mountain of God; you walked in the midst of the stones of fire. You were blameless in your ways from the day you were created, until unrighteousness was found in you. By the abundance of your trade you were internally filled with violence, and you sinned; therefore, I have cast you as profane from the mountain of God. And I have destroyed you, O covering cherub, from the midst of the stones of fire.
Ezekiel 28:14-16

After losing his residence in heaven, Satan was next seen in the Garden of Eden, where he deceived man *(Genesis 3:1-13)*, causing him to rebel against his Creator and drawing the line of battle between the two kingdoms—the kingdom of Light and the kingdom of darkness.

As one Bible scholar states: "Satan is a creature; he is no match for the Creator. Satan is powerful, but not omnipotent. He can hinder, but he cannot prevent. The master of deceit can convince the prayer warrior that his or her prayer has not reached the Throne. Your strength is to remember that Satan is a defeated antagonist. To accredit it to him otherwise is to allow Satan supremacy over you. He is—and always will be—the Usurper. You cannot avoid warfare. You are continuously involved in the battle. Therefore, you must 'Draw near to God, resist the devil (stand your ground) and he will flee.'"

Let us examine some of Satan's names recorded in Scripture so that you can better understand the character of your enemy. Many of his names not only reveal his character, but also suggest his tactics in warfare against the Body of Christ.

* **devil**
  Matthew 4:1,5,8,11; 1 John 3:8,10; Jude 9; Revelation 12:9,12; 20:2

* **father of lies**
  John 8:44

* **god of this evil world**
  2 Corinthians 4:4

* **an infidel or unbeliever**
  2 Corinthians 6:15

* **prince of the bottomless pit or angel of the abyss (destroyer)**
  Revelation 9:11

* **angel of light**
  2 Corinthians 11:14

* **star of the morning, son of the dawn**
  Isaiah 14:12

* **the enemy or the avenger**
  Psalm 8:2

* **evil one**
  Matthew 6:13; John 17:15

* **adversary**
  1 Peter 5:8

* **ruler of demons (Beelzebub)**
  Matthew 12:24

* **the destroyer**
  Job 15:21; 2 Thessalonians 2:3

* **the accuser**
 Revelation 12:10

* **the tempter**
 Genesis 3:1; Matthew 4:3; 1 Thessalonians 3:5

* **the dragon**
 Revelation 12:7-13; 20:2

* **the serpent**
 Genesis 3:1-4,13; Revelation 12:9; 20:2

* **the deceiver**
 Genesis 3:13; 2 Thessalonians 2:3

What are his tactics?

To convince the world that he does not exist.

To blame men and circumstances instead of himself.

To lay claim to the principalities (Christ referred to him as the prince of this world).

To use his rule which is limited to:

- This time, not the hereafter
- The world, not heaven
- The people in darkness, not the children of light

To perpetuate spiritual sins, which are subtle.

To fight not for trivial things, but for heaven itself.

How does he really fight?

As stated earlier, Satan uses your mind by accusing you and judging you; then he keeps you in that position by guarding over you.

He raises doubt through suggestion such as: "You are not a Christian, look at what you did yesterday." "You aren't really saved," or "You can't give the exact date that you accepted Jesus." "Look at you, you have a past."

He creates fear: "These times you live in are hopeless." "What if you get cancer?"

He steals from you financially: car problems, water heater breaking, air conditioner going out, losing your job, etc.

Satan also uses your fear of man: "Everybody will laugh at you if you talk about Jesus." "What will people think if ...?" When you become a God pleaser more than a man pleaser, one of your biggest battles is won.

What is your strategy?

First of all, recognize that to fight Satan, you must fight in the realm of the spirit. Spiritual things are spiritually discerned, not figured out by human reasoning. You are not fighting flesh and blood, but the powers of darkness.

Be alert to cycles or patterns in attacks from the enemy—a rash of accidents, sicknesses that lead to death. DON'T FEAR, you have all authority and power in the name of Jesus. (See "Weapons of Warfare.")

You may wonder, "If Jesus won the battle, why are we fighting?" Let's look at the end of World War II. Even though the victory was won and Hitler was defeated, occupation troups remained in different areas of the nations. It is the same with you; you must maintain the victory that was won at Calvary through the blood of Jesus.

RECOGNIZE THE PLACE OF BATTLE

Scripture teaches that man is a tripartite being, made up of body, soul, and spirit:

> Now may the God of peace Himself sanctify you entirely; and may your spirit and soul and body be preserved complete, without blame at the coming of our Lord Jesus Christ.
>
> *1 Thessalonians 5:23*

In the soulish realm—the seat of the intellect, emotions and will—the mind is the most common battleground of man, for it is in the mind that choices are made. These choices, all of which involve the will, determine not only the course of a man's daily life, but also his eternal destiny.

As the Word of God becomes alive in you and you act upon it, the Word will change your heart and mind, and your actions will change for your good and for God's glory. Through Christ, the believer can receive revelation and understanding of spiritual mysteries, whereas the unbeliever is spiritually blind. (Compare *Ephesians 1:17-21* and *4:17,18*.)

Scripture clearly teaches that Jesus has defeated Satan—stripped him of his power—and put all things under Christ's feet *(Ephesians 1:19-22)*. The enemy's primary point of attack is against your mind, to raise questions—as he did in tempting Eve in the garden and Jesus in the wilderness—to influence you to doubt God's Word and His faithfulness.

Your mind has three voices to which it may

respond: God's, the enemy's, and your own. The more you become familiar with God's Word, the easier it will be for you to recognize God's voice, for He always speaks that which is consistent with His character, as revealed in His Word. The voice of the Holy Spirit will speak to provide encouragement, comfort, direction, revelation, assurance of God's love, conviction or correction.

By contrast, the enemy usually speaks in such a way as to bring thoughts of doubt, guilt, fear, jealousy, hatred, self-condemnation or self-righteousness. Your own "self-talk" is usually based on your human logic and reasoning, or your selfish desires and will.

You must take authority over the voice of the enemy and forbid him to speak—"Submit yourselves therefore to God. Resist the devil and he will flee from you" *(James 4:7).* Bind your own voice of human reasoning and desire, then open your mind and spirit to receive the voice of the Holy Spirit. Often the direction for prayer which the Holy Spirit gives does not seem logical to the human mind; do not allow this to hinder your obedience and effectiveness.

Spiritual things must be spiritually discerned—not figured out by human reasoning. Affirm the truth of Paul's teaching: "I have the mind of Christ." *(See 1 Corinthians 2:14-16.)*

Recognize that your fight is not with flesh and blood, but with the powers of darkness and Satan's spiritual rulers of this age. This age (world) has become the battleground between these satanic forces and mankind. Therefore, you are not fighting against people you know or with whom you come in contact in your daily life. The enemy may harass you by stirring up strife in the lives of people who are close to you in order to deter you from prayer and intercession. Always remember that the real battle is in the spiritual realm, and not in your physical circumstances.

Satan sends assignments against your spirit, soul, and body. If he can keep you oppressed, he can keep you from growing spiritually and from being an effective intercessor. Taking authority over the enemy and making the right choices according to God's Word will bring you into victory and increase your spiritual growth. Failure to make the right choices gives ground to physical sickness, emotional problems, and stunted spiritual growth.

STRATEGY FOR WARFARE

The work of the intercessor is to combat the enemy in the spirit realm (as opposed to the natural realm), using spiritual weapons (not carnal ones). In the process, he or she must determine strategy for warfare through the guidance and revelation of the Holy Spirit. *Discernment* is a key element in your strategy, and a vital quality for leaders and intercessors to possess. To discern means "to distinguish or separate." God said to His prophet Jeremiah, "If you extract the precious from the worthless, you will become My spokesman" *(Jeremiah 15:19).*

Activity in the heavenlies is intensifying as the time of the Messiah's sure return draws near. Intercessors seem to be saying with one voice, "The conflict is real, and the battle lines are being drawn!" As spiritual warfare intensifies, particularly in the area of the mind, the intercessor's prayer life must not falter.

Satan doesn't fight fair in this battle. If he can't keep you from praying at all, he will assail you with doubt, discouragement and fear as you look at seemingly impossible circumstances. This deceiver will try to make you feel you are being objective and getting a lay of the land as you look at the situation. In reality his goal is to sideline you with an attitude of hopelessness and passivity.

You need to know your enemy! General Douglas McArthur, when stating some important requisites of military victory, gave the following:

* A will to win—a cause worth dying for.

* Strength—adequately trained and well-equipped personnel.

* Adequate source of supply—lifelines must be kept open.

* Knowledge of the enemy—"The greater the knowledge of the enemy, the greater the victory."

The same is necessary for maintaining your victory. Jesus has won the victory. It is your place to "occupy until (He) come(s)."

Let's look at Nehemiah and see how he overcame the battle of the mind.

The Lord put it in Nehemiah's heart to rebuild the wall around Jerusalem. As he fasted and prayed over the situation, God gave him favor with the king. The king released him to go back to his homeland to rebuild the city wall.

How did Satan fight that? By waging a battle in Nehemiah's mind. First, he attacked his reputation by trying to make a mockery of his efforts, saying, "What they are building—if even a fox climbed up on it, he would break down their wall of stones"

(Nehemiah 4:3).

When mockery and discouragement failed to deter Nehemiah, the next thing the enemy tried was intimidation and fright. Nehemiah knew the enemy was trying to render him helpless through fear.

Then the enemy (in the form of two men) sent word, "Come, let us meet together in one of the villages on the plain of Ono" *(Nehemiah 6:2).* With this he recognized a major principle in warfare: "Never negotiate with the enemy!" Though this threatening message was sent to him FIVE times, Nehemiah steadfastly refused to negotiate on enemy territory.

This warrior builder also resisted the advice of a false prophet who tried to get him to run and hide from the enemy. He prayed from God's perspective, and fearlessly moved on to fulfill the commission God had given him.

Satan still tries to lure you into his encampment through the mind, just as he tried to do with Nehemiah. There is no mention of battle, only that which was done through the battle of the mind. You are defeated the moment you come down to the enemy's level.

Satan and his ruling spirits give specific assignments to the fallen angels—or demons—in his army. They will seek to manipulate circumstances and people in order to carry out their assignments. However, as a believer you have the power and the authority to thwart their success and to destroy their assignments and curses. Not only that, you can turn those curses back upon the ranks of the enemy to do greater damage to Satan's cause than he intended for the body of believers. *(See Acts 13:6-12.)*

A study of Scripture indicates that Satan has delegated spiritual rulers to be in charge of countries and geographical areas. Read *Ezekiel 28* and chapters 9 and 10 in *Daniel* for an example of how strongholds operate over a geographical area. Keep in mind that the spiritual warfare takes place in the heavenlies, but the effects of that warfare are seen upon the earth and in people's lives.

Consider the story of an evangelist in Latin America who was passing out tracts and witnessing to people on the streets of a particular city. A provincial boundary ran through the heart of the city. The evangelist met great opposition from the people with whom he tried to share the gospel; they threw the tracts in the gutter and refused to listen to his message.

In frustration, the evangelist crossed to the other side of the street, which was in a different province and under a different government. Suddenly he realized the attitude of the people on this side of the street was completely different—though their language and outward appearance were the same as the first group of people he had encountered. These people gladly accepted the gospel tracts, and eagerly listened to his message of salvation.

Sometime later the evangelist learned that a group of Christians in the second province had been binding the forces of darkness in their area, and praying for the gospel to go forth. Because of their spiritual warfare, the work of the evangelist was fruitful. But apparently no one was waging warfare on behalf of the first province, and resistance to the gospel was very strong.

In Daniel's experience, the "prince of the kingdom of Persia" withstood the angel whom God had sent with the answer to the prophet's prayers *(Daniel 10:12,13)*. When Daniel prayed, his prayers brought additional reinforcements into the spiritual conflict, and the prince of Persia was overcome. Daniel influenced the entire nation of Israel through his fasting and his persistent prayer.

Ask the Lord for specific revelation and discernment concerning the leaders for whom you are praying, and for the areas in which they are ministering. In praying for those who work among Moslems or in an area where cults are prevalent, you will be combatting an antichrist spirit. Where occult activity is strong, you are dealing with spirits of deception, control, and seduction, as well *(1 John 2:18)*.

In an area where there are many churches, but much conflict among the leaders and members, the Holy Spirit may reveal to you that the problem is a religious spirit ruling over that area, along with spirits of strife, contention and self-righteousness. Discerning the spirits responsible for a given problem—if indeed evil spirits are responsible—will make your intercession more specific and more effective.

Be alert to certain patterns or cycles in attacks from the enemy. For some period of time there have been strong attacks against marriages among spiritual leaders. One particular denominational group has lost a large number of missionaries to cancer. Then there was a rash of serious accidents causing death or severe injury to ministers and missionaries, and/or their family members. The intercessors should serve as "watchmen on the wall" to help ward off these attacks through spiritual warfare, and lend their support by praying for those on the front lines of ministry.

PUT ON YOUR SPIRITUAL ARMOR

Since you are engaged in a spiritual battle, it is

only wise to be acquainted with the armor of God which secures your safety and allows you to withstand the attacks of the enemy in these evil days.

> Finally, be strong in the Lord, and in the strength of His might. Put on the full armor of God, that you may be able to stand firm against the schemes of the devil. For our struggle is not against flesh and blood, but against the rulers, against the powers, against the world forces of this darkness, against the spiritual forces of wickedness in the heavenly places.
>
> Therefore, take up the full armor of God, that you may be able to resist in the evil day, and having done everything, to stand firm. Stand firm therefore, having GIRDED YOUR LOINS WITH TRUTH, AND HAVING PUT ON THE BREASTPLATE OF RIGHTEOUSNESS and having SHOD YOUR FEET WITH THE PREPARATION OF THE GOSPEL OF PEACE; in addition to all, taking up the SHIELD OF FAITH with which you will be able to extinguish all the flaming missiles of the evil one. And take THE HELMET OF SALVATION, and the SWORD OF THE SPIRIT, which is the word of God. With all prayer and petition pray at all times in the Spirit, and with this in view, be on the alert with all perseverance and petition for all the saints.
>
> *Ephesians 6:10-18*

The armor written about in *Ephesians 6* is compared to that of a Roman soldier. A common complaint of the soldiers was that the armor was very heavy. Without proper exercise and discipline, the armor became weighty and would cause a soldier to lay it aside, leaving him undisciplined for battle and unprotected from the enemy.

In the realm of the spirit, your spiritual armor

fulfills the same function that the physical armor fulfilled for the Roman soldier. You are called daily to walk with Christ. You must be disciplined not only to put on the armor, but to wield your weapons in battle against the forces of darkness. Your armor is to be a defense against the strategy of the devil so as to protect you from assault. The sword of the Spirit (God's Word) is an offensive weapon to attack, overpower, and plunder the spoil of the powers of darkness. Lack of exercise and discipline will leave you open to assault. Therefore, be diligent as a soldier of God's army, always wearing your armor and ready for battle.

It might also help you to keep in mind that the Roman soldier was expected to be in full-time service to his commanders. Paul makes reference to this in writing to Timothy:

> No soldier in active service entangles himself in the affairs of everyday life, so that he may please the one who enlisted him as a soldier.
> *2 Timothy 2:4*

This symbolizes the Christian's loyalty to Jesus Christ, the Commander-in-Chief, living a life of single-minded allegiance to Him.

Romans 13:12,14 says: "So let us lay aside the deeds of darkness and put on the armor of light...put on the Lord Jesus Christ." Your spiritual armor is, in reality, the Lord Jesus Christ. He wants to be your defense by clothing you in Himself. You walk in total security when you walk daily covered in Jesus. Unlike conventional armor, your spiritual armor should never be taken off!

WHY DO YOU NEED TO
DAILY WEAR THE ARMOR?

* It helps you to stand against the schemes of the devil.

* It keeps you strong in the Lord and in the power of His might.

* It enables you to resist in the evil day of the enemy's attack.

* It secures your safety and repels the enemy.

* It accomplishes the Father's will.

On the next few pages you will find a chart on each piece of the Armor of God, beginning with Standing Firm and ending with The Whole Armor of God. You will see each Area of Protection, including the Definition and Application, the Affirmation (Scriptures) and the Declaration. When the enemy attacks, refer to the page where the appropriate piece of armor is listed. Read the Scriptures given and repeat the declaration.

STANDING FIRM

Area of Protection	Affirmation	Declaration
DEFINITION To STAND means to resist without yielding; to maintain a position; to persist; to endure; to remain upright; to encounter; to meet face to face.	2 Chronicles 20:15,17 Joshua 1:9	Having done all, I am going to stand firm. I will not yield to the devil's schemes, but will hold fast to the Word of God.
APPLICATION As an heir and child of God, you are to STAND in that place that is already yours. It has been delivered to you through the cross of Jesus Christ.	1 Corinthians 16:13 Ephesians 6:11-14	I will stand in faith on the solid rock, Jesus. You are my foundation; I will not be moved by the roar of the enemy, nor by negative circumstances. I will stand valiant and strong, for with You on my side, who can be against me?
Do not in any way surrender to an uprising of the enemy. Submit yourself to God; then STAND and resist the devil and he will flee.	Philippians 4:1	As a priest before You, O Lord, I will bless Your Holy name and serve You in obedience.
Note: Jesus did not use the Word of God to attack the devil; He used it to maintain the victory He already had.	1 Thessalonians 3:6-8 2 Thessalonians 2:1-5	I will stand in the victory that has been won, for the battle is not mine but Yours. In this way, I am more than a conqueror in Christ Jesus.

THE GIRDLE OF TRUTH

Area of Protection	Affirmation	Declaration
DEFINITION LOINS are a picture of strength, power, vigor, and maturity. They include the reproductive organs, the digestive system and the bowel. Weak loins disable a soldier. THE GIRDLE, worn about the loins to brace him for the fight, was a symbol of a soldier's strength and superior ability. It kept the armor in place, and supported the sword; money and valuables were also carried here. To GIRD means to prepare oneself for action.	Exodus 12:11 Deuteronomy 33:11 Psalm 51:6; 69:23 Luke 12:35 John 14:6	Jesus, You are my truth. You have made me to know the truth in my inward parts. I am dressed in readiness because Your truth clothes me. I encompass my mind with Your truth so I am ready for action. I resist all double-mindedness, and claim that I have the mind of Christ.
APPLICATION One whose mind is girded with truth will be strong and vigorous with mature spiritual insight, and will reproduce the Word of God for His glory. One who is double-minded is unstable in all his ways. TRUTH is the teaching presented in God's Word, embodied in Jesus Christ, revealed to us by the Holy Spirit. WE GIRD OURSELVES WITH TRUTH when we embrace and uphold God's revelation to us, and walk in agreement with Him.	1 Corinthians 2:16 Ephesians 4:15; 6:14 2 Thessalonians 2:13 2 Timothy 2:15 James 1:8; 4:8 1 Peter 1:13	I shall know the truth and the truth will set me free. I will speak forth the truth in love today. I will accurately handle the Word of truth, and will plant seeds of truth in others so that You may be reproduced in them. Thank You, Jesus, for choosing me from the foundation of the world for salvation through sanctification by the Spirit and faith in the truth.

THE BREASTPLATE OF RIGHTEOUSNESS

Area of Protection	Affirmation	Declaration
DEFINITION The BREASTPLATE, covering the soldier's vital organs (heart, lungs, liver, etc.), came down over the girdle, increasing the protection of the loins. By protecting these vital organs, the breastplate emboldened a soldier to face the enemy without fear.	Proverbs 28:1 Isaiah 59:16-17 Romans 3:22,25,26 Romans 5:17-19	Jesus, You are my righteousness. In You I live and move and have my being. Help me to conform to Your character and Your will in my life. I put on Your righteousness by faith and ask that You protect my heart, that I may walk with pure motives.
APPLICATION RIGHTEOUSNESS — right-standing or uprightness before God—is imparted by Christ to the believer. This BREASTPLATE OF RIGHTEOUSNESS preserves the Christian's soul and conscience—the "vital organs" of his spirit-man. Thus he is filled with courage, knowing he is protected by the righteousness of Christ and can face the enemy without fear.	2 Corinthians 5:21 Ephesians 6:14 1 Thessalonians 5:8 1 John 1:7,9	Help me to do that which is right and just, so that I might have a clear conscience and not be afraid of evil consequences. Thank You for courage to face the enemy without fear. Thank You for cleansing me from my sins and restoring me to fellowship with You because You were the perfect sacrifice for my sins.

THE SHOES OF THE GOSPEL OF PEACE

Area of Protection	Affirmation	Declaration
DEFINITION The phrase "preparation of the gospel of peace" means "to be ready, or dressed in readiness," which was vital when a soldier had to dodge, stand, or run in hand-to-hand combat with the enemy. His SHOES had metal cleats, which made him more sure-footed in battle.	Exodus 12:11	Jesus, You are my peace. You have brought to my life wholeness and harmony with the Father. May Your peace sanctify me wholly«body, soul and spirit.
	1 Samuel 2:9	
	Psalm 18:33	
	Psalm 66:8,9	I shod my feet with Your gospel, Your peace. I desire to walk today in a quiet, unquarrelsome manner. Thank You for keeping my feet from harm, and guiding my path.
APPLICATION FEET represent your walk with the Lord. Your "walk" is the witness of your speech, your behavior and your attitude. SHOD means to bind under or to tie up; i.e., to be ready to receive marching orders. Shoes were removed upon entering a house, and put on again when going out. GOSPEL is the good news that Jesus Christ was crucified for our sins, was raised from the dead, and has defeated the enemy. PEACE is freedom from strife«inner peace which comes from God though conflict with the enemy rages without. It is a walk founded in reconciliation.	Isaiah 26:3	
	Matthew 12:18-20	My feet will not be moved from the gospel, for I am not ashamed of the good news. Your gospel is the power of God for salvation to everyone who believes.
	Romans 1:16	
	Ephesians 6:15	
	Colossians 1:20	Because my feet are set securely in Your peace, I am ready to maneuver in any direction the Holy Spirit leads me. Keep me in a state of readiness so that I can boldly tread upon enemy territory to set the captives free from Satan's bondage.
	1 Thessalonians 5:23	

THE SHIELD OF FAITH

Area of Protection	Affirmation	Declaration
DEFINITION THE SHIELD, a defensive weapon, was usually carried on the left arm and was used to protect the entire body of a soldier. The surface was kept bright with oil, which reflected the sun to blind the enemy. It helped deflect the enemy's blows.	Proverbs 30:5 Jeremiah 1:12 2 Corinthians 5:7 Galatians 2:20	Lord Jesus, You are my shield of faith. My self nature has been crucified with You, and the life I now live, I live by faith in You. I will resist the devil by being firm in that faith. Thank You for being a shield unto me. I put my trust in You, choosing to walk by faith, not by sight or circumstances. I will speak words of faith and I will ask in faith without doubting.
APPLICATION A SHIELD represents protection and security; our shield of faith works in cooperation with the other pieces of armor to quench the fiery darts of doubt, fear and unbelief, and to blind the enemy. The mind and the will control its movements. FAITH is simply believing, accepting and appropriating what God has said. FAITH requires a total trust in the Lord Jesus in all things.	Ephesians 6:16 Colossians 1:10,11 Hebrews 10:22; 11:1 James 1:6; 4:7 1 Peter 1:5; 5:9 1 John 5:10	Your Word is Your power. Thank You, Father, that You are alert and active, watching over Your Word to perform it. It protects me from the evil one because … "It is written." The devil runs in terror from me because I draw near unto You and resist him in Jesus' name by lifting up this shield of faith which is anointed with the oil of Your Holy Spirit.

THE HELMET OF SALVATION

Area of Protection	Affirmation	Declaration
DEFINITION The HELMET was the armor worn by a soldier to protect his head. It often bore insignia or ornaments identifying the army to which the soldier belonged.	Psalm 140:7 Isaiah 51:6; 59:16,17 Romans 8:6; 12:2	Jesus, You are my salvation. You have covered my head in the day of battle; You are my strength and song and You have become my Salvation.
APPLICATION The HELMET, the hope of salvation, guards your mind from the enemy's darts. Your mind directs the use of your shield and your sword and all movements of the body; thus it must be protected so that you can be an effective soldier.	2 Corinthians 2:16; 10:5 Ephesians 4:23; 6:17 Colossians 3:2	I put my hope and trust in You. The helmet of hope shall be as a helmet of deliverance to me. You have set my mind free from the darts of the enemy.
Your mind is the battleground between the flesh and the spirit; a disciplined soldier will not yield to the flesh, but will be strong in spirit.	1 Thessalonians 5:8 Titus 1:2; 3:7 Hebrews 5:9 1 Peter 1:13	Today I will renew my mind by the Word of God; I refuse to entertain the thoughts of doubt and unbelief the enemy would bring to me. I bring every thought into captivity to the obedience of Christ. I will concentrate on those things which pertain to life and peace. All praise be unto You, the God of my Salvation!

THE SWORD OF THE SPIRIT

Area of Protection

DEFINITION
The SWORD was both defensive and offensive. It defended the soldier from the enemy's assault, and was used to wound or kill the enemy. It was wielded with the right arm, and was a symbol of power and authority.

APPLICATION
The SWORD OF THE SPIRIT is the Word of God quickened and made alive by the Holy Spirit; the wielding of this sword is only effective when the other pieces of armor are in place.

The WORD comes from your mouth. The Word of God is your power and authority when quickened by the Holy Spirit. It will judge the thoughts and intents of your own heart, and of the heart of the one spoken to.

Affirmation

1 Samuel 17:54

Psalm 149:6

Jeremiah 15:16

Luke 21:15

John 1:1,14

1 Corinthians 1:30

Ephesians 6:17

Hebrews 1:3; 4:12

Declaration

Lord Jesus, You are the Living Word. I go forth with praises in my mouth and a two-edged sword in my hand. Today I will confess Your Word before men, and You will confess me before the Father in heaven. Your words are true. Your Word is the foundation of the world. You are the joy and rejoicing of my heart because I have been called by Your name, and therefore have the authority to use this weapon. I will to speak forth Your Word in power. Your Word abides in me and I in You.

Your Word is quick and powerful and sharper than any two-edged sword; it divides between that which is spiritual or godly, and that which is soulish or of the flesh. Your Word is Your wisdom. The Holy Spirit will give me in the hour of need a mouth of wisdom which none of my opponents will be able to resist or refute.

Thank You, Lord Jesus, for giving me the provision of Your Word, my SWORD!

THE WHOLE ARMOR OF GOD

When the enemy attacks in these areas, refer to the page where the appropriate piece of armor is listed. Read the scriptures given and repeat the declaration.

Type of Attack	Protection	Type of Attack	Protection
Lies against the character of God Deception about who I am Error as to the way I am going	Girdle of Truth	Having trouble with thoughts of guilt, condemnation, hatred towards others Operating in flesh and not the spirit Remaining in darkness; unrenewed mind	Helmet of salvation
Believing accusations from Satan Feeling condemned Puffed up with spiritual pride	Breastplate of righteousness	Whispered words like "Hath God said?" Distortion of the Word of God Word taken out of heart of the hearer Listening to doctrines of demons	Sword of the Spirit
Attacked by persecution or lies Compromising the Word of God Passive and asleep	Feet shod with gospel of peace		
Hit by a flaming missile of doubt, fear, or unbelief	Shield of Faith		

WALKING IN TRIUMPH

With your armor of God in place, know that it is in and through Christ Jesus alone that you triumph.

> But thanks be to God, who always leads us in His triumph in Christ, and manifests through us the sweet aroma of the knowledge of Him in every place. For we are a fragrance of Christ to God among those who are being saved and among those who are perishing.
>
> *2 Corinthians 2:14,15*

According to James M. Freeman *(Manners and Customs of the Bible*, pp. 460,461), a Roman military procession of triumph was one of the spectacular events of ancient times. It was granted to a conqueror when he had met all the qualifications of victory established by the Roman Senate. One of these qualifications was that the victory be complete and decisive, putting an end to war. In this victory NO enemy could remain.

On the day chosen for the triumphal procession, people crowded into the streets and onto buildings to get a good view of the conqueror in whose honor it was held. This procession was made up of the conqueror, the senate members, heads of state, chief citizens and the prisoners who had been captured. The valuable spoils of the war were prominently displayed.

The conqueror, wearing a robe embroidered with gold, and a tunic covered with flowers, rode in a special chariot drawn by four horses. In his right hand he held a laurel wreath which was the symbol of the crown of a conqueror; in his left hand he held a scepter.

It was a day when all the heathen temples were open and decorated elaborately with sweet-smelling flowers. Incense was lit on every altar so that the victor was greeted with a cloud of perfume.

Paul uses this analogy in writing about the believer being victorious in Christ Jesus. In *2 Corinthians 2:14,15*, Paul thanks God who ALWAYS leads us in triumph. Christ Himself is the conqueror; we are trophies of His victory. Our prayers and our lives diffuse a sweet odor of Him wherever we go.

The following verses also refer to this analogy:

> When He [God] had disarmed the rulers and authorities, He made a public display of them, having triumphed over them through Him [Christ].
>
> *Colossians 2:15*

> And when He had taken the book, the four living creatures and the twenty-four elders fell down before the Lamb, having each one a harp, and golden bowls full of incense, which are the prayers of the saints.
>
> *Revelation 5:8*

Intercession is an incense before God's altar, and the prayers of the righteous do accomplish much. It is through intercession that the battle is won over the forces of darkness. You must constantly wear the armor of God to be able to withstand and overcome during this war.

On that day when the seal is broken in heaven and the trumpet sounds, may your prayers return unto Him as sweet-smelling incense before His throne. And may you be a fragrance of Christ unto God among those being saved and among those who are perishing.

WEAPONS
OF WARFARE

WEAPONS OF WARFARE

TEXT:

> For though we walk in the flesh, we do not war according to the flesh, for the weapons of our warfare are not of the flesh, but are divinely powerful for the destruction of fortresses. We are destroying speculations and every lofty thing raised up against the knowledge of God, and we are taking every thought captive to the obedience of Christ, and we are ready to punish all disobedience, whenever your obedience is complete.
>
> *2 Corinthians 10:3-6*

As you come to God on behalf of others, there will be times you will need to battle against the powers of darkness.

It is God's will for us to tear down strongholds in people's lives and loose them in areas in which they have not been able to freely function. This is a primary purpose of the spiritual weapons God provides for us. As we war on earth, it stirs divine intervention from heaven.

The following diagram helps you to visually grasp the complete arsenal of spiritual weapons every believer has at his or her disposal. The pillars which support this arsenal are Faith and Obedience, and Praying in the Spirit; these are essential for the effective implementation of the seven primary weapons. God has provided all that is necessary for successful spiritual warfare; your part is to *will* to use the weapons His Word guarantees will destroy enemy strongholds.

In warfare there are four possible attitudes—offense, defense, detente, and desertion...Satan can get along very well with Christians as long as they are on the defensive, seeking detente, or deserting. Therefore, if we are determined to see him defeated in our own hearts and in our society, we must be only and always committed to the offensive.

—Arthur Mathews, *Born for Battle*, p. 51

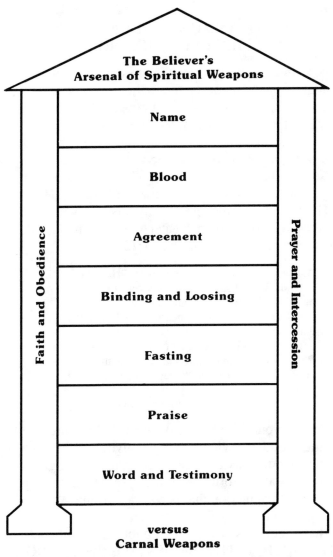

The Believer's Arsenal of Spiritual Weapons

Name

Blood

Agreement

Binding and Loosing

Fasting

Praise

Word and Testimony

Faith and Obedience

Prayer and Intercession

versus
Carnal Weapons

Mind (Human Reasoning)
Soul (Human Desire)
Will

Manipulation
Deception
Control

FAITH AND OBEDIENCE—
OUR PILLAR OF VICTORY

These two factors go together to comprise one of the pillars which supports the believer's arsenal of spiritual weapons. Faith and obedience are so intertwined that one is incomplete without the other.

You must have FAITH that the weapons God provides for you will work and accomplish the desired purpose for His glory. Have FAITH in the name of Jesus. Have FAITH in the power of Jesus. Have FAITH that the same power dwells in you and empowers you to do even greater works than He did, because Jesus lives in you *(John 14:12)*.

> And Jesus answered saying to them, "Have faith in God. Truly I say to you, whoever says to this mountain 'Be taken up and cast into the sea,' and does not doubt in his heart, but believes that what he says is going to happen, it shall be granted him. Therefore, I say to you, all things for which you pray and ask, believe that you have received them, and they shall be granted you."
>
> *Mark 11:22-24*

Exercise your faith by speaking forth the Word and declaring aloud the victory Christ gives. When the Holy Spirit quickens a verse of scripture for a given situation, speak it forth as a word of faith, casting down every imagination that is contrary to the Word of God *(2 Corinthians 10:5)*.

What quenches all fear, doubt and unbelief? FAITH, FAITH, FAITH. BELIEVING, BELIEVING, BELIEVING.

You can speak forth FAITH as a command. Note the example in *Acts 16:18,* "But Paul was greatly annoyed, and turned and said to the spirit, 'I command you in the name of Jesus Christ to come out of her.' And it came out at that very moment."

The importance of OBEDIENCE—which also includes commitment—cannot be overemphasized. As an intercessor, your work is going to be constant and challenging. You will be putting yourself in the place of the person for whom you are praying, sometimes feeling his or her need. This type of prayer calls for obedience to the voice of the Spirit and unwavering commitment. But a word of warning: *Do not allow intercession to keep you burdened.* Learn how to respond in obedience when the Spirit calls you to prayer, then release prayer burdens to your loving heavenly Father.

Commitment means the act of entrusting to: delivered in trust. Therefore, your commitment and determination to withstand the enemy and aggressively oppose him will strengthen your warfare. The enemy recognizes this quality in you. Someone has aptly said that all hell trembles to see a saint on his knees. For this very reason, the enemy will try to keep you from prayer. Your obedience and commitment will foil his plan!

As a Christian you are set apart and consecrated to God for His sacred purpose. As you entrust your LIFE to Him more and more every day, the world will notice a difference.

> And they overcame him because of the blood of the Lamb and because of the word of their testimony, *and they did not love their life even to death.*
>
> *Revelation 12:11*

Your LIFE is now hidden with Christ in God (*Colossians 3:3*). Since He laid down His LIFE for you; you should lay down your LIFE for the brethren (*1 John 3:16*).

> It is a trustworthy statement: For if we died with
> Him, we shall also live with Him; if we endure,
> we shall also reign with Him; if we deny Him,
> He also will deny us; if we are faithless, He
> remains faithful, for He cannot deny Himself.
>
> *2 Timothy 2:11-13*

PRAYER AND INTERCESSION—
THE PILLAR OF COMMUNICATION
AND POWER

We have already discussed in previous chapters the importance of communication with God and the difference between prayer and intercession. Prayer and intercession comprise the other pillar which supports the arsenal of spiritual weapons.

In this section we will discuss the matter of praying in the spirit. The term praying in the spirit can mean different things to different people or denominations.

To some it means following the leading of the Holy Spirit and praying as He directs you in your understanding or in song. As you pray earnestly you follow the prompting of the Spirit deep within your spirit.

These prayers may be prayed from the heart or from written prayers such as *My Utmost for His Highest* by Oswald Chambers, *Prayers that Avail Much* by Word Ministries, Inc. or the prayers in the section of this book titled Daily Prayers.

To others it may mean praying in an unknown tongue. This is not to be confused with the gift of tongues. The gift of tongues is to be used in conjunction with the gift of interpretation.

> When you assemble...If anyone speaks in a tongue,
> it should be by two or at the most three, and each in
> turn, and let one interpret; but if there is no

interpreter, let him keep silent in the church; and
let him speak to himself and to God.
1 Corinthians 14:26-28

As you look at the following scriptures you will
see that this form of praying in the spirit can also be a
tool for some intercessors.

1. **PRAYING IN THE SPIRIT IS YOUR SPIRIT
   COMMUNICATING DIRECTLY WITH
   GOD.** It is primarily for use in your devotional
   prayer life for intercession, praise and worship.

   > ...let him speak to himself and to God.
   > *I Corinthians 14:28b*

   > For one who speaks in a tongue does not speak
   > to men, but to God; for no one understands, but
   > in his spirit he speaks mysteries.
   > *I Corinthians 14:2*

2. **PRAYING IN THE SPIRIT IS A PERFECT
   PRAYER.** Since you do not always know how
   or what to pray in a given situation, you can
   bring the need before the Lord by praying in
   the spirit. The Holy Spirit, your Helper,
   enables you to pray as you ought thereby
   praying in the Lord's will.

Praying in the spirit is a means by which the
Holy Spirit intercedes through your spirit in
prayer. This is where we get the term "prayer
language," an unlearned language in which you
can pray. When you pray with your
understanding you are easily influenced by
your feelings, thoughts, desires, experiences,
distractions, understanding and will. Even
your vocabulary can limit your prayers. God
gives you a prayer language that bypasses your

mind, will and emotions and allows you to continue in prayer without interruption.

> And in the same way the Spirit also helps our weakness; for we do not know how to pray as we should, but the Spirit Himself intercedes for us with groanings too deep for words; and He who searches the hearts knows what the mind of the Spirit is, because He intercedes for the saints according to the will of God. And we know that God causes all things to work together for good to those who love God, to those who are called according to His purpose.
>
> *Romans 8:26-28*

> For if I pray in a tongue, my spirit prays, but my mind is unfruitful.
>
> *I Corinthians 14:14*

> And this is the confidence which we have before Him, that if we ask anything according to His will, He hears us. And if we know that He hears us in whatever we ask, we know that we have the requests which we have asked from Him.
>
> *I John 5:14,15*

> You ask and do not receive, because you ask with wrong motives...
>
> *James 4:3*

3. **PRAYING IN THE SPIRIT HAS DEFINITE MEANING.** Although you do not understand what you are praying, God does.

> There are, perhaps, a great many kinds of languages in the world, and no kind is without meaning.
>
> *I Corinthians 14:10*

4. **PRAYING IN THE SPIRIT EDIFIES THE PERSON PRAYING.** When you are built up,

strengthened and encouraged, you can continue with the spiritual warfare you are called to do.

> One who speaks in a tongue edifies himself...
> *I Corinthians 14:4a*

> But you, beloved, building yourselves up on your most holy faith; praying in the Holy Spirit.
> *Jude 20*

5. PRAYING IN THE SPIRIT HAS THE AUTHORITY OF HEAVEN BEHIND IT.

There is no way you could know when Satan and his demonic forces will launch an attack. The Holy Spirit will prompt you at the strategic, opportune time.

> With all prayer and petition pray at all times in the Spirit, and with this in view, be on the alert with all perseverance and petition for all the saints.
> *Ephesians 6:18*

> For our struggle is not against flesh and blood, but against the rulers, against the powers, against the world forces of this darkness, against the spiritual forces of wickedness in the heavenly places.
> *Ephesians 6:12*

> ...for the effective prayers of a righteous man can accomplish much.
> *James 5:16b*

Praying is an act of your will, whether you are praying in the spirit or with your understanding. When Peter walked on the water he had to exercise his will and faith. He got out of the boat and he moved his feet. Walking was not the miracle. The fact that he didn't sink was.

Praying in the spirit is similar. You must respond to the Holy Spirit's prompting in the same way. Speaking is not the miracle. The fact that you speak in a language you don't understand is. The Holy Spirit will give you the utterance. Just as with any language, the more you use it, the more comfortable you become.

If you pray in tongues it is important that you do not criticize, condemn or exclude those who don't. On the other hand, it is just as important to remember, if you do not pray in tongues, that you refrain from the same attitudes or judgments. The issue is not how you pray, but that you are faithful to the call of prayer and led by the Spirit.

The Apostle Paul wrote, "I thank God, I speak in tongues more than you all...Now I wish that you all spoke in tongues...Do not forbid to speak in tongues" *(I Corinthians 14:5,18,39)*.

Communication with the Lord through prayer and intercession is a pillar on which our life in Christ depends. It is a strong pillar of support in the Christian's arsenal of spiritual weapons against the enemy. Praying and singing in the spirit is the power that moves mountains and draws you into fellowship with the Lord.

> What is the outcome then? I shall pray with the spirit and I shall pray with the mind also; I shall sing with the spirit and I shall sing with the mind also.
>
> *I Corinthians 14:15*

THE NAME OF JESUS— OUR AUTHORITY

The name of JESUS has power in earth, heaven and hell. Since you are a temple of His Spirit and the same Holy Spirit dwells in you, you can take His name and use it just as though He Himself were here. "I have given you authority over all the power of the enemy," Jesus promised *(Luke 10:19)*.

Jesus gave His followers power and authority over demons, and He gave them the right to ask the Father for things in His name.

> And whatever you ask in My name, that will I do, that the Father may be glorified in the Son. If you ask Me anything in My name, I will do it.
> *John 14:13,14*

> Therefore also God highly exalted Him, and bestowed on Him the name which is above every name, that at the name of Jesus every knee should bow, of those who are in heaven, and on earth, and under the earth.
> *Philippians 2:9,10*

Everything has to bow at the name of Jesus. So use the name of JESUS during warfare. God recognizes it. So do the devil and his hosts. Make the enemy flee in terror. Say the name of our Lord Jesus.

Here is an effective way to pray using Jesus' name and authority:

> By the authority of Jesus and His precious blood, I bind you, Satan, according to Ephesians 6:12 and break your powers over this situation. I loose <u>(name of person)</u> from your hold and destroy your works and your assignment in Jesus' name.
>
> Father, I ask that Your will now be done, and I thank you. In Jesus' name and by His authority, I declare it done.

The power of the Holy Spirit in you gives you authority to use the name of Jesus to defeat the enemy. It can be likened to a policeman who can halt a huge truck just by standing in the middle of the highway and holding up his hand to signal, "Stop!" The policeman, wearing his badge, has authority behind him to stop traffic and forbid the truck to proceed if a law has been violated. Intercessors, too, must use their delegated authority to stop demonic forces from wreaking havoc with God's people.

> But the one who joins himself to the Lord is one spirit with Him.
>
> *1 Corinthians 6:17*

> ...that He would grant you, according to the riches of His glory, to be strengthened with power through His Spirit in the inner man...
>
> *Ephesians 3:16*

> But if the Spirit of Him who raised Jesus from the dead dwells in you, He who raised Christ Jesus from the dead will also give life to your mortal bodies through His Spirit who indwells you.
>
> *Romans 8:11*

A key to your authority to use the name of Jesus is your personal relationship with Him. That relationship, nurtured by your time of fellowship with the Lord, ensures that you will use this authority *only* in ways that will glorify Him. Note the example of Peter and John speaking to the lame man at the temple gate in *Acts 3:1-8*. On the other hand, note what happened to those who tried to use the name of Jesus without proper authority *(Acts 19:11-17)*. If you are walking in proper relationship to Jesus Christ, the enemy must submit to your authority when you use the name of Jesus.

"And these signs will accompany those who have believed: in My name they will cast out demons, they will speak with new tongues; they will pick up serpents, and if they drink any deadly poison, it shall not hurt them; they will lay hands on the sick, and they will recover."

Mark 16:17,18

THE BLOOD OF JESUS— OUR COVERING

And not through the blood of goats and calves, but through His own blood, He entered the holy place once and for all, having obtained eternal redemption. For if the blood of goats and bulls and the ashes of a heifer sprinkling those who have been defiled, sanctify for the cleansing of the flesh, how much more will the blood of Christ, who through the eternal Spirit offered Himself without blemish to God, cleanse your conscience from dead works to serve the living God?

Hebrews 9:12-14

What the blood of Jesus does for us:

* Gives SALVATION. Births us into His Kingdom and keeps us from eternal damnation *(Mark 16:16; John 3:3,17)*.

* Makes ATONEMENT for us, blotting out sins *(Leviticus 17:11; Romans 5:11)*.

* REDEEMS us. Our life is paid for in full, bought back from the power of sin and death *(Psalm 107:2; Ephesians 1:7; Hebrews 9:12; Revelation 5:9)*.

* JUSTIFIES us. Acquits us of sin and guilt *(Acts 13:38,39; Romans 5:9)*

* Makes us RIGHTEOUS. Puts us back into right standing with God *(Isaiah 59:2; Romans 3:22,23,25; 1 John 1:9).*

* Gives SANCTIFICATION. Sets us apart unto God at the time of salvation as well as each day thereafter through the blood of Jesus *(1 Corinthians 1:30; Hebrews 10:10,14).*

* Allows REMISSION of sins. Sin was cancelled *(Romans 3:24,25; Hebrews 9:22).*

* RECONCILES us. Accepting God's provision, we can now fellowship with Him in love *(Romans 5:10; Colossians 1:20).*

* Gives OVERCOMING POWER as we receive and use what has been delegated to us *(Luke 10:19; Revelation 12:11).*

* Provides DELIVERANCE. Releases from powers of darkness and sets us free *(2 Corinthians 2:14; Colossians 1:13).*

* FORGIVENESS. Pardons sins *(Colossians 1:14; 1 John 1:9).*

* NEW COVENANT. Replaces old covenant of sacrifices; perfect sacrifice now has been made through Jesus Christ *(Hebrews 7:22; 8:13; 9:15; 10:9; 12:24).*

* CLEANSES from all sin *(1 John 1:7).*

"Pleading the blood of Jesus" is a tactic for intercession used by prayer warriors over the years. Because of abuse, it has become somewhat controversial. To "plead the blood of Jesus" over a person for his or her protection is simply to remind the enemy of his boundaries. It is the same principle we see in *Exodus 12:22,23* when the blood of the lamb on the doorposts meant the death angel could not touch that household.

The blood of Jesus secures lasting peace and victory. A foreshadowing of this is seen in *1 Samuel 7:3-14*. In this account Samuel challenged Israel to destroy the false gods of the Philistines which they had allowed to pollute the land. The people responded in obedience and observed a day of fasting. The Philistines were angered when they heard their idols had been destroyed, so they staged an attack. The people said to Samuel, "Do not cease to cry to the Lord our God for us, that He may save us from the hand of the Philistines" (v. 8). Samuel responded by taking a suckling lamb and offering it as a whole offering to the Lord.

In his book, *Born for Battle,* Arthur Mathews sums up the account:

> Standing identified with the complete acceptance of his lamb, Samuel cries unto the Lord for Israel. The Lord thunders from heaven, the Philistines are frightened off, and, according to the record, "came no more into the coast of Israel."

> The victory was necessary to the peace. Peace is victory sustained. The only man who can keep the enemy at bay is the intercessor, and blessed is that intercessor who knows how to use the power of the blood in spiritual warfare.

"Precious blood, by this we conquer
In the fiercest fight,
Sin and Satan overcoming
by its might."

—F. R. Havergal
(Mathews, p. 63)

AGREEMENT—OUR BONDING

As an intercessor you AGREE with the Holy Spirit on that which He has called you to accomplish through spiritual warfare. Agreement means "to harmonize, to live in concord, without contention." We are all called to be consistent with our prayers by the Word and by the Spirit.

If you are going to learn to pray in agreement, you have to learn to be in one accord with another intercessor. "When the day of Pentecost had come, they were all together in one place" *(Acts 2:1)*. The believers were all in one accord.

You may want to work with a prayer partner or partners in some of your intercession. Such an alliance with someone of like spirit can strengthen your warfare. Choose such a prayer partner very carefully under the direction of the Holy Spirit; human logic must not be the determining factor in such a choice. However, if it is just one partner, the person should be of your same sex, and should be accessible for frequent communication. If you feel the Lord is leading you to a specific individual to be a prayer partner, and the feeling is mutual, test the relationship. Is the relationship pure, holy and above reproach, and are there any hidden motives? Would the Lord be pleased?

Jesus said:

> Again, I say to you, that if two of you agree on
> earth about anything that they may ask, it shall
> be done for them by My Father who is in
> heaven. For where two or three have gathered
> together in My name, there I am in their midst.
>
> *(Matthew 18:19,20)*

And Solomon records:

> A threefold cord is not quickly broken.
>
> *(Ecclesiastes 4:12, KJV)*

Learning to pray in agreement is learning to pray
in God's will. As your mind is transformed, you will
discover the perfect will of God and be in agreement
with Him through His Word. (Read *Romans 12:2.*)

There is a warning about what could happen if you
are in agreement over something ungodly. Read *Acts
5:1,2* and *9*, and you will see that when Ananias and
his wife Sapphira agreed to tell a lie, their plot cost
them their lives. "Why is it that *you have agreed
together to put the Spirit of the Lord to the test?*"
Peter asked Sapphira just before she fell over dead.

You may ask, "What if I make a mistake?" If your
heart is right and your motives pure, God's grace will
abound.

Learn to discern the spirit of the one with whom
you are agreeing. If you agree with the word of the
enemy—by listening to bad reports he whispers in
your ear or sends by way of someone else—you are in
wrong agreement. Agree with what the Word tells you
or the Holy Spirit brings to your mind.

Invite the Holy Spirit to be present before you
even start to pray. Pray in one accord with Him.

BINDING AND LOOSING—OUR KEYS

BINDING and LOOSING are two effective weapons given by Jesus to His followers.

> I will give you the keys of the kingdom of heaven; and whatever you shall bind on earth shall have been bound in heaven, and whatever you shall loose on earth shall have been loosed in heaven.
>
> *Matthew 16:19*

What then is the meaning of the phrase, "shall be bound in heaven...shall be loosed in heaven?" One Bible translator points out that the verb form is the perfect passive participle, *so the reference is to things in a state of having been already forbidden (or permitted).* This tells us that whatever is bound or loosed by the believer is done on the basis that it has already been done "in heaven."

> Or how can anyone enter the strong man's house and carry off his property, unless he first binds the strong man? And then he will plunder his house.
>
> *Matthew 12:29*

The context of this passage finds Jesus casting out demons. The Greek word for "bind" in the verse means "to fasten or tie—as with chains—as an animal tied to keep from leaving."

Binding and loosing is not some kind of spiritual magic and cannot be used at every whim, such as, "Satan, I bind you off of my lottery ticket." This is an example of improper binding. It is contrary to the Word of God and would be for selfish purposes. It has nothing to do with binding and loosing for kingdom purposes.

One author has this to say about binding and

loosing. "It has to do with the authority of the Christian in spiritual warfare, and there are often many factors involved. Binding and loosing is a confident assurance and confession of God's order and government over against the disorder of a sin-cursed, demonized world."

The Dictionary of New Testament Theology says, "The idea of binding may also refer back to the picture of the binding of the strong man (that is, Satan) who must first be bound before his goods (that is, those enthralled by him) may be plundered *(Matthew 12:29 Parallel; Mark 3:27; see also Luke 11:21)*. Thus Peter would be promised the power that Christ had to bind the powers of evil and to liberate men, and this would hold good not only on earth, but also in heaven (Vol. 2, p.733)."

In order to bind the strong man, you must first know who the strong man is. It can be a principality, power, ruler of darkness in this world or a spiritual wickedness in high places *(Ephesians 6:12)*. This is discerned through prayer and must always be within the will and timing of God. Many times fasting must accompany that prayer. When the man asked Jesus why His disciples could not cast the demon out of his son, He replied, "But this kind does not go out except by prayer and fasting" *(Matthew 17:14-21)*.

Every individual believer has the right and authority to call down or resist the devil and bind the strong man. You as an individual will be singled out and challenged by the spirits of darkness. Or you will be called into war against the powers over your home, church, city, etc.

Binding and loosing demonic spirits or powers of higher-level spiritual dominion is definitely something you do not want to do without knowledge of what you are doing. When calling down strongholds, you may assist one in prayer and agreement as you learn, but never work alone. You must know your spiritual jurisdiction.

There can be serious repercussions if this is done outside of the realm of authority directly related to the order and authority of the Church. The heirarchy of darkness *(Ephesians 6:12)* understands authority and the chain of command of God's people. Moving without the proper authority is very dangerous to you and can create havoc within the church, etc., in which you are ministering.

To what then does the LOOSING refer? To setting the captive free! Do you recall the story of Jesus healing the woman who had a spirit of infirmity for 18 years? Jesus told her, "Woman thou art loosed from thine infirmity." (See *Luke 13:11,12 KJV.*)

The Greek word for "loose" is defined in the lexicon as "to loose anything tied or fastened; to loose one bound; to set free; to discharge from prison. To free from bondage or disease (one held by Satan) by restoration to health."

James M. Freeman, in his book *Manners and Customs of the Bible,* explains the common usage in the Jewish schools of the words "bind" and "loose." To "bind" is to "forbid," and to "loose" is to "allow." Binding and loosing is prohibiting and permitting. In the Aramaic language, which Jesus used, it was a customary expression to denote the highest authority.

Jesus gave Peter the keys of the kingdom of heaven. When Jesus asked Peter who He was, Peter said, "Thou art the Christ, the Son of the living God" *(Matthew 16:16).* Then Jesus went on to say, "...upon this rock (revelation) will I build my church; and the gates of Hades shall not overpower it. I give you the keys of the kingdom of heaven: whatever you shall bind on earth shall be bound in heaven, and whatever you shall loose on earth shall be loosed in heaven." Not only did Jesus give the keys to Peter, He gave them to His Church as well.

To BIND is to secure the enemy with pressure so he cannot move. To LOOSE is to gain liberty using the Word of God. Binding refers to the enemy, while loosing refers to the victory.

There is no formula for binding and loosing, it must be done by revelation of His Spirit; however, here is an example of the way you might pray in dealing with the devil concerning a loved one:

> I speak to you, Satan, in the mighty and precious name of Jesus Christ of Nazareth. I take authority over you and bind all demonic spirits assigned to _____. Loose _____ and let him go free in the name of Jesus. I demand that you stop your maneuvers against this child of God. _____ is covered by the blood of Jesus, the precious Lamb slain for him. (You might bind anything the Lord speaks to your heart as you pray. The Spirit of the Lord will lead you.)

> Lord, I ask that Your will now be done, and I thank You. In Jesus' name and by His authority, I declare it done.

> Thank You, Lord, for watching over Your Word to perform it, in Jesus' name.

FASTING—OUR CUTTING EDGE

Fasting—our cutting edge—is most often done in secret and coupled with prayer. More than just abstaining from food, it is an act of self-denial for higher purposes. It is important to check your motives and heart attitudes with the Lord before you determine to pray with fasting.

> And whenever you fast, do not put on a gloomy face as the hypocrites do; for they neglect their appearance in order to be seen fasting by men. Truly I say to you, they have their reward in full. But you, when you fast, anoint your head, and wash your face so that you may not be seen fasting by men, but by your Father who is in secret; and your Father who sees in secret will repay you.
>
> *Matthew 6:16-18*

Notice that Jesus did not say "if" you fast, but "when" you fast. He expected Christians to use that discipline in their prayer lives. What is FASTING? It is the voluntary and deliberate abstinence from food for the purpose of concentrated prayer. Jesus dealt with our motives for fasting and said we should never fast to impress others.

Being full of the Holy Spirit does not necessarily mean you walk in the power of the Spirit. One way into power is fasting and prayer *(Luke 4:1,2,14)*, which makes you much more spiritually sensitive to the Word of God and hearing His voice. This sensitivity to the Holy Spirit causes more power in your life to combat the forces of Satan.

When the bridegroom is taken away, the disciples fast *(Matthew 9:14,15)*; it is a spiritual discipline *(2 Corinthians 6:5)*.

Fasting, which is shown in the New Testament as a means of gaining direction from the Holy Spirit, gives clarity of mind and spirit. (See *Acts 13:1-3; 14:21-23.*)

What is accomplished in FASTING? Probably more than you will ever know until you get to heaven.

> Is this not the fast which I chose, to loosen the bonds of wickedness, to undo the bands of the yoke and to let the oppressed go free, and break every yoke?
>
> *Isaiah 58:6*

> Consecrate a fast, proclaim a solemn assembly; gather the elders and all the inhabitants of the land to the house of the Lord your God, and cry out to the Lord.
>
> *Joel 1:14*

Why pray with FASTING?

* Jesus set an example by spending 40 days fasting in the desert *(Matthew 4:2; Luke 4:2).*

* As a freewill offering to the Father, it pleases Him *(1 Samuel 7:5,6; Acts 14:23).*

* It produces a spiritual and physical discipline *(Luke 2:36,37; 1 Corinthians 9:26,27).*

* It keeps you from God's judgments *(Joel 2:12-14; Jonah 3:5-8).*

* It manifests concern for family, church, community and country *(2 Samuel 1:12; 12:16; Ezra 8:21; Esther 4:3,16; Daniel 9:3; Matthew 9:15; Mark 2:18-20; Luke 5:33-35).*

Benefits from FASTING:

* Strengthens and implements prayer *(Acts 10:30,31)*.

* Brings blessings of obedience *(Matthew 6:6,16)*.

* Brings humility through repentance *(Nehemiah 9:1-3)*.

* Gives revelation of God's way and will for your future *(Daniel 9)*.

* Establishes authority and power in prayer and spiritual warfare *(Matthew 4:1-11)*.

Fasting brings great victories. Example: King Jehoshophat called a national fast against invading armies, and the enemies killed each other *(2 Chronicles 20:1-30)*.

Fasting gives you a proper mental attitude: You should not view fasting as punishment, even though your body may rebel at first.

FASTING SHOULD BE VIEWED AS A PRECIOUS OPPORTUNITY TO GET CLOSER TO THE LORD, not distracted by the daily focus of eating. God responds to your sincerity when you willingly humble yourself.

Ways to FAST:

* <u>Twenty-four hour fast</u>. From sunset to sunset. Abstain from solids.

* <u>Partial fast</u>. Abstain from pleasant foods. Partake only of clear soups, fruit juices, cereals

or grains, OR, give up one meal a day for prayer. *(See Daniel 1:8-16 and 10:2,3.)*

* <u>Three-day fast</u>. Total abstinence of food for three days. (See example in *Esther 4:16.*)

* <u>Extended fast</u>. Has two methods; both require preparation. Before an extended fast, it is recommended you omit caffeine and rich foods from your diet.

 * <u>Total fast</u>—excludes all food but does include water. Fast should be broken slowly. Only diluted juices for a day or two. Next gradually proceed to fruits, vegetables, and grains, adding meats last.

 * <u>Non-total fast</u>—no food intake, but diluted fruit juices, water and hot herbal teas are taken.

IF YOU ARE ON MEDICATION, CONSULT YOUR PHYSICIAN BEFORE COMMENCING AN EXTENDED FAST. You may need to consider a partial fast only. Fast when directed by the Holy Spirit and according to your disciplined prayer life *(Isaiah 58:6; 1 Corinthians 9:26,27).*

Use your fast as an opportunity to pray more. During this time your spirit is much more sensitive to the Holy Spirit, and you often will receive keener revelation from God's Word. Fasting is not an endurance test nor a religious ritual. It is a privilege and blessing to approach the Lord in humility and whole-hearted faith.

Scriptures on FASTING:

Exodus 34:28	Moses
Leviticus 16:29-31	Day of Atonement
Leviticus 23:27-32	Day of Atonement
1 Samuel 1:7,8	Hannah's prayer
2 Samuel 12:16-23	David for Bathsheba's child
1 Kings 13:8-24	Elijah
1 Kings 19:8	Elijah's journey to Horeb
1 Kings 21:27	By Ahab in self-humiliation
2 Chronicles 20:3	Proclaimed by Jehoshaphat
Ezra 8:21-23	Proclaimed by Ezra
Nehemiah 1:4	By Nehemiah
Nehemiah 9:1	People of Jerusalem confessing sin
Esther 4:16	Called by Esther
Job 33:19,20	As a result of sickness and pain
Isaiah 58	Fasting which pleases God
Jeremiah 14:12	That which is unacceptable
Joel 2:12	Returning to God with whole heart
Matthew 6:16-18	Not as hypocrites do
Matthew 17:21	Only by prayer and fasting
Luke 2:37	Anna worshiping in temple
Luke 4:2	Jesus' 40-day fast
Luke 18:12	Self-righteous and boastful
Acts 9:9	Saul of Tarsus
Acts 10:30	Cornelius when angel appeared
Acts 13:2,3	By prophets and teachers in Antioch
Acts 14:23	At appointment of elders
Romans 14:21	Abstaining for sake of weaker one
1 Corinthians 7:5	In marriage relationship
2 Corinthians 6:5	Ingredient of Apostolic ministry

(from *God's Chosen Fast*, by Arthur Wallis)

You should see a fast as a means by which your prayers may be more perfectly focused. Fast with a definite goal, thus breaking the bondage and opposition of Satan. Concentrate on Jesus in prayer when you fast, making time in your schedule for communion with Him.

BEFORE ATTEMPTING A PROLONGED FAST, BECOME VICTORIOUS WITH THE SHORTER ONES, SUCH AS A ONE-DAY FAST OR A PARTIAL FAST.

PRAISE—OUR BANNER

PRAISE is an important key in spiritual warfare, and one of the most powerful weapons available to the believer. Jesus set the example of PRAISE by teaching the disciples to start and end their prayers with PRAISE. Don't wait to win the victories before you start PRAISING; it will lay the groundwork for the victories the Holy Spirit desires. You actually do battle from a position of victory *(Ephesians 1:20-22)*. Look at the example of Paul and Silas:

> And when they had inflicted many blows upon them, they threw them into prison, commanding the jailer to guard them securely; and he, having received such a command, threw them into the inner prison, and fastened their feet in the stocks. But about midnight Paul and Silas were praying and singing hymns of praise to God, and the prisoners were listening to them; and suddenly there came a great earthquake, so that the foundations of the prison house were shaken; and immediately all the doors were opened, and everyone's chains were unfastened.
>
> *Acts 16:23-26*

> And a voice came from the throne, saying, "Give praise to our God, all you His bond-servants, you who fear Him, the small and the great."
>
> *Revelation 19:5*

My mouth is filled with Thy praise, and with
Thy glory all day long.

Psalm 71:8

Let everything that has breath praise the Lord.

Psalm 150:6

What does PRAISE do?

* It blesses the Lord *(Psalm 66:8; Luke 24:52,53)*.

* It brings you into His presence and draws you closer to Him *(Psalm 100:4)*.

* It opens doors and makes rough places smooth *(Isaiah 60:18; Acts 16:25,26)*.

* It defeats the devil *(2 Kings 11:13,14; Psalm 149:5-9)*.

* It brings revival *(2 Chronicles 31:2; 34:12; Psalm 107:32)*.

   *It keeps you happy and gives you joy *(Isaiah 61:1-3; Acts 2:45-47)*.

Praise is an act of body worship. Have you ever considered that when you worship God you are expressing a variety of emotions with your body?

Examples of body worship through PRAISE:

* When you clap your hands and stomp your feet, you portray your excitement *(2 Kings 11:12; Psalm 98:8; Isaiah 55:12; Lamentations 2:15; Ezekiel 6:11)*.

* When you stand up, march or walk, you portray readiness to serve or to go (*Genesis 13:17; Deuteronomy 11:22-25; Joshua 1:1-5; Psalm 68:7,8*).

* When you lift up your hands, you are worshiping and surrendering to God (*Exodus 17:8-16; 1 Kings 8:22-24; Psalms 28:2; 63:3,4; 134:2; 141:2; Luke 24:50,51; 1 Timothy 2:8; Hebrews 12:12*).

* When you dance, you express great joy (*1 Samuel 18:6,7; Psalms 30:11; 149:3; Jeremiah 31:13; Luke 15:11-24*).

* When you sing, you express gladness of heart (*Psalms 68:25; 100:2; 108:1; Proverbs 29:6; Isaiah 26:19; 65:13,14; Jeremiah 31:7; Zechariah 2:10; 1 Corinthians 14:15; James 5:13; Revelation 15:3*).

* When you play skillfully on an instrument, you show forth adoration (*1 Samuel 16:23; 18:6,7; 1 Chronicles 15:28; 16:42; 25:1,3,6; 2 Chronicles 5:13,14; 34:12; Psalm 33:3*).

* When you fall prostrate (to fall down flat in homage to royalty or God), you portray deep emotion and total surrender to God (*Psalm 72:11; Isaiah 45:14*).

* When you kneel, you are portraying humility and dependence upon God (*2 Chronicles 6:13; Matthew 17:14; Mark 1:40*). Kneeling is asking for mercy (*Luke 22:41; Acts 9:40; 21:5*).

* When you sit down or keep silent, you show

forth rest and trust in God *(Exodus 14:14;
Joshua 6:10; Job 2:13; Proverbs 13:3; 17:27;
Amos 5:13; Matthew 8:4; 12:16; 27:14; Luke
23:9; John 8:6).*

THE WORD OF GOD AND OUR TESTIMONY—
OUR FOUNDATION

This weapon is mentioned last, not because it is
least important, but because it is the foundation upon
which the entire arsenal rests. Everything you do in
spiritual warfare must be based on the Word of God.

Words work for you or work against you. Learn to
use them as Jesus did. It is His Word abiding in you
that causes faith to be present in your words *(John
15:7,8).*

> And take the helmet of salvation, and the sword
> of the spirit, which is the word of God.
> *Ephesians 6:17*

> For the word of God is living and active and
> sharper than any two-edged sword, and piercing
> as far as the division of soul and spirit, of both
> joints and marrow, and able to judge the
> thoughts and intentions of the heart.
> *Hebrews 4:12*

You can learn to use God's Word against the devil
just as Jesus did when tempted by him. He replied, "It
is written...it is written...it is written." Each time He
quoted God's Word, and He was victor *(Matthew
4:4,7,10; 10:32).*

When you confess God's Word aloud as your
affirmation, Jesus confesses you before the Father.
The more you know and confess the Word, the more

effective the victory will be. You must have a storage of scripture in your spirit to use when needed.

Another effective way to use the Word as a weapon is to establish a "document of confirmation" based on the word the Lord has given for a particular situation. A document of confirmation is a most valuable weapon of spiritual warfare.

According to Webster's dictionary, a document is "a lesson, a proof, anything printed, written, relied upon to record or prove something. Anything serving as proof, to prove or support, as by reference to documents."

Let's look at some documents in the Bible:

God told Moses on Mount Sinai to document His words to Israel by writing them on tablets. God considered them so important that when Moses later broke them, God immediately rewrote them with His finger. These we know as The Ten Commandments.

> Then the Lord said to Moses, write down these
> words, for in accordance with these words I
> have made a covenant with you and with Israel.
> *Exodus 34:27*

When His people returned from captivity to Jerusalem, Nehemiah commanded them to renew their covenant relationship with God. "Now because of all this we are making an agreement in writing; and on the sealed document are the names of our leaders, our Levites and our priests" *(Nehemiah 9:38)*.

God told Ezekiel to write a document of war, revealing to Ezekiel the heart of King Nebuchadnezzar to launch an all-out attack against

Jerusalem. God instructed Ezekiel to mark the date down so that he would know later what God had told him was the truth.

> And the word of the Lord came to me in the ninth year, in the tenth month, on the tenth of the month saying, "Son of man, write the name of the day, this very day. The king of Babylon has laid seige to Jerusalem this very day."
>
> *Ezekiel 24:1,2*

The prophet Habakkuk was commanded by the Lord to record the vision which had been given him as a witness in the end-time.

> Then the Lord answered me and said, "Record the vision and inscribe it on tablets, that the one who reads it may run. For the vision is yet for the appointed time; it hastens toward the goal, and it will not fail. Though it tarries, wait for it; for it will certainly come, it will not delay."
>
> *Habakkuk 2:2,3*

A document of confirmation is an article in writing that gives a word of testimony or promise, and usually has a date and a signature.

Many intercessors have found it helpful to keep a prayer journal to record words they receive from the Lord during their prayer time. God holds these words in high esteem; He will stand behind them to bring them to pass if they are in line with His Word and will. (See "Journaling.")

A document of confirmation can be a passage of scripture which He quickens to your spirit during your fellowship with Him. It can also be a direct word from the Lord revealed through a prophecy by the Holy Spirit. It may even be something the Lord reveals as He allows you to interpret what you have prayed in the spirit. It will *always* be in alignment with God's Word, and consistent with God's character.

However you receive a word, write down the declaration and record the date. Later you will be blessed when remembering how God gave you that miracle which He promised you, or when you see the word come to pass.

You may use your Sword of the Spirit in these ways:

1. Quote the Word to the enemy to remind him of his defeat.

2. Quote the Word to the Lord to affirm His promises that you are claiming on someone's behalf.

3. Ask the Lord to give you a word for direction for the person or situation for which you are interceding. (Example: In praying for someone with a serious illness, the Lord may give a word, with a verse such as, "This sickness is not unto death..." [John 11:4 KJV]. Then write it down and remain steadfast in prayer until the answer comes.)

4. Allow the Holy Spirit to quicken the Word to you for encouragement and correction, and to give guidance and strategy for your intercession.

NAMES OF GOD—OUR COVENANT

The Word of God admonishes all His people to "call upon His name." To do this more effectively, it helps to understand His attributes.

The next few pages are notes taken from *Names of God*, by Nathan J. Stone. You will better understand God by knowing the provisions He has made for you as found in the examples of His name. May it also enrich your prayer life as you begin to refer to Him by some of His mighty names.

ELOHIM:

Triune creator; sovereign of the universe, and life, and of all nations; who covenants to preserve His creation.

General idea of greatness, glory, creative and governing power, omnipotence, sovereignty, creator of the universe.

Elohim is mainly concerned with the *creation* and preservation of the world and His works. He assumes a great love toward all creation and creatures as the work of His hands.

Plural, representing the Trinity, under obligation of an oath to perform certain conditions.

EL:

Mighty, strong, prominent, "God," great, dreadful, "Almighty God."

EL SHADDAI:

The God who is "all-sufficient" and "all-bountiful," the One who fills and makes fruitful, used in connection with judging, chastening, purging, translated "almighty."

EL SHADDAI first appears in connection with Abraham in *Genesis 17:1 (KJV):* "And when Abram was ninety years old and nine, Jehovah appeared to Abram, and said unto him, 'I am EL SHADDAI (God Almighty!)'" At this time Abram's name was changed to Abraham because he understood the revelation of EL SHADDAI as the One with whom all things were possible.

ADONI:

Sovereign Lord, master of our lives, sir, owner. Implies a claim upon man's obedience and service.

ADONI reveals the relationship which God sustains toward us and what He expects of us. ADONI is used hundreds of times in relation to Jesus Himself. We are not our own, we have been bought with a price. We belong to ADONI: spirit, soul, and body.

ADONI also represents the One who bestows gifts upon and equips His servants for service. We His servants are to be His inheritance, the portion and possession of His people.

JEHOVAH:

The being who is absolutely self-existent, possesses eternal life and permanent existence, eternal and unchangeable, the self-existent God of revelation.

JEHOVAH is known as the God who expresses Himself in essential moral and spiritual attributes. JEHOVAH reveals His love as conditioned upon moral and spiritual attributes. JEHOVAH places man under moral obligations with a warning of punishment for disobedience.

JEHOVAH is derived from the Hebrew verb "havah" meaning "to be" or "being." It is the name most frequently employed in the Old Testament, occurring 6,823 times.

There are eight compound names of JEHOVAH in the Old Testament. *These names were used when JEHOVAH wanted to make a special revelation of Himself.*

1. JEHOVAH-JIREH (jī' ra)
   "Jehovah's provision shall be seen"

2. JEHOVAH-RAPHA (rä' fa)
   "Jehovah heals"

3. JEHOVAH-NISSI (nis' sē)
   "Jehovah my banner"

4. JEHOVAH-MEKADDISH (ma ka dish')
   "Jehovah who sanctifies"

5. JEHOVAH-SHALOM (sha lōm')
   "Jehovah is peace"

6. JEHOVAH-TSIDKENU (tsid kā' nu)
   "Jehovah our righteousness"

7. JEHOVAH-SHAMMAH (shäm mah')
   "Jehovah is there"

8. JEHOVAH-ROHI (rō e')
   "Jehovah my shepherd"

There is a wonderful and significant order in these compound names of JEHOVAH as they appear in Scripture. There is a progressive revelation of Jehovah providing for each need as it arises—saving, sustaining, strengthening, sanctifying. The order in which these eight names appear shows JEHOVAH'S purpose to meet the developing spiritual and physical needs of His people Israel.

JEHOVAH-JIREH:
"Jehovah's provision shall be seen"

And Abraham said, "God will provide for Himself the lamb for the burnt offering, my son." So the two of them walked on together. ...And Abraham called the name of that place The Lord Will Provide, as it is said to this day, "In the mount of the Lord it will be provided."

Genesis 22:8,14

DEFINITION: It shall be seen, it shall be provided; sense of foreseeing, seer, prophet.

JEHOVAH-JIREH is a kind of seeing that is different from Elohim, all knowing. This kind of seeing means *foreseeing is prevision*. Prevision is the noun form of "seeing beforehand." Thus to God, prevision is followed with provision. FOR HE WILL CERTAINLY PROVIDE FOR THAT NEED WHICH HIS FORE-SEEING SHOWS TO EXIST. With Him prevision and provision are one and the same thing.

The name JEHOVAH-JIREH arose out of the instance of Jehovah's provision of a substitute for Isaac, whom He had commanded Abraham to sacrifice upon the altar. The name stands for *Jehovah's great provision for man's redemption in the sacrifice of His only begotten Son, Jesus.* He is the Lamb of God who takes away the sin of the world, who was offered up on the very spot where Abraham had predicted— "in the mount of the Lord it will be provided."

JEHOVAH-JIREH is to us the one who provides the sacrificial Lamb of God for our redemption.

JEHOVAH-RAPHA:
"Jehovah heals"

> Then Moses led Israel from the Red Sea, and they went out into the wilderness of Shur; and they went three days in the wilderness and found no water. And when they came to Marah, they could not drink the waters of Marah, for they were bitter; therefore, it was named Marah. So the people grumbled at Moses, saying, "What shall we drink?" Then he cried out to the Lord, and the Lord showed him a tree; and he threw it into the waters, and the waters became sweet. There He made for them a statute and regulation, and there He tested them. And He said, "If you will give earnest heed to the voice of the Lord your God, and do what is right in His sight, and give ear to His commandments, and keep all His statutes, I will put none of the diseases on you which I have put on the Egyptians; for I, the Lord, am your healer."
>
> *Exodus 15:22-26*

DEFINITION: To restore, to heal, to cure in a physical and spiritual sense.

The Lord Jesus consummated His ministry by becoming THE TREE which made the bitter pools of human existence waters of life. The teaching of Marah is wonderfully fulfilled in Him. *Jesus is both the tree and the waters.* He bore our sins in His body on the tree, and is also our Well of Salvation. Only Jesus, the tree of God's provision, purifies, sweetens, and heals man's bitter experiences in life. He heals the diseases of the soul and of the body.

JEHOVAH-NISSI:
"Jehovah my banner"

And Joshua did as Moses told him, and fought against Amalek; and Moses, Aaron and Hur went up to the top of the hill. So it came about when Moses held his hand up, that Israel prevailed, and when he let his hand down, Amalek prevailed. But Moses' hands were heavy. Then they took a stone and put it under Him, and he sat on it; and Aaron and Hur supported his hands, one on one side and one on the other. Thus his hands were steady until the sun set. So Joshua overwhelmed Amalek and his people with the edge of the sword. Then the Lord said to Moses, "Write this in a book as a memorial, and recite it to Joshua, that I will utterly blot out the memory of Amalek from under heaven." And Moses built an altar, and named it The Lord is My Banner; and he said, "The Lord has sworn; the Lord will have war against Amalek from generation to generation."

Exodus 17:10-16

DEFINITION: The Lord our Banner, a sign of deliverance and salvation, the standard of our victory in life's conflicts.

A banner is translated: pole, ensign, standard; among the Jews it is also a word for miracle.

It was a sign to God's people to rally to Him. The banner stood for His cause, His battle.

The banner of Jehovah held aloft in Moses' upraised hands brought victory to His people. This is always assured to the people of God—victory over the powers of evil, the enemy of our souls—when His banner is over us.

Isaiah predicts a rod to come forth out of the stem of Jesse. This stem or root is also a sign, a banner to the people. The stem of Jesse is Jesus, born of the seed of David according to the flesh. Jesus is our banner of redemption, our banner of welfare.

With Jehovah-Jesus as our banner, we may go from strength to strength giving thanks to God, "who always leads us in His triumph in Christ Jesus..." *(2 Corinthians 2:14).*

JEHOVAH-MAKADDISH:
"Jehovah who sanctifies"

> You shall consecrate yourselves therefore and be holy, for I am the Lord your God. And you shall keep My statutes and practice them; *I am the Lord who sanctifies you.*
>
> *Leviticus 20:7,8*

DEFINITION: To set apart, sanctify or hallow, to dedicate, to consecrate, to be holy.

The Book of Leviticus explains how a redeemed people should walk worthy of their calling and participate in the spiritual worship which Jehovah demands of them. In connection with Israel's moral and spiritual purity, this title JEHOVAH-M'KADDESH is repeated many times in Leviticus.

In the Old Testament the word "sanctify" was used to set apart places, furnishings, people and special days. The people of Israel were set apart to God and separated from all other people.

Jesus was from His very conception set apart by the power of the Holy Spirit. He was altogether holy, spotless and without sin. Jesus became our High Priest, and in His redeeming love, He was made sin for us *(Luke 1:35; 2 Corinthians 5:21; Hebrews 4:15; 7:26).*

Jesus became our Sanctification *(1 Corinthians 1:30; Hebrews 10:10,14).*

To such holiness, or separateness, we have been

elected *(Ephesians 1:4)*. Holiness is a positive and active word. The people of God must be holy in practice as well as separated in position. The one is meaningless without the other. It is the church's glorious destiny to be presented holy and spotless to her Lord.

JEHOVAH-SHALOM:
"Jehovah is peace"

> When Gideon saw that he was the angel of the Lord, he said, "Alas, O Lord God! For now I have seen the angel of the Lord face to face." And the Lord said to him, "Peace to you, do not fear; you shall not die." Then Gideon built an altar there to the Lord and named it The Lord is Peace. To this day it is still in Ophrah of the Abiezrites.
>
> *Judges 6:22-24*

DEFINITION: Peace, wholeness, finished, making good a loss, welfare, well-being, perfect, deepest desire of the human heart. In the Hebrew language it also means harmony of relationship or a reconciliation based on the completion of a transaction, the payment of a debt, the giving of satisfaction.

PEACE OFFERING: A sacrifice, the shed blood of which provided atonement on which reconciliation and peace were based *(Leviticus 3; 7:11-21)*. Peace is broken by sin. Peace offerings restored fellowship between God and man.

Jesus is the Prince of Peace who was promised to us in the Old Testament. While on earth, Jesus preached and promised peace. He healed, comforted and commanded the people to go in peace.

Jesus made peace for us through the blood of the

cross. Our peace in Him is measured by our ability to keep trusting Him and by our sanctification. Peace depends on trust and obedience. If we are carnally minded we will lack peace. Therefore, let us allow peace to rule in our hearts *(Philippians 4:7,9; Colossians 1:20; 3:15)*. There is no peace apart from Jesus, for individuals or for nations.

JEHOVAH-TSIDKENU:
"Jehovah our righteousness"

> Behold, the days are coming, declares the Lord, When I shall raise up for David a righteous Branch; and He will reign as king and act wisely and do justice and righteousness in the land. In His days Judah will be saved, and Israel will dwell securely; and this is His name by which He will be called, "The Lord our Righteousness."
>
> *Jeremiah 23:5,6*

DEFINITION: Rendering justice and making right; to justify, declare innocent, or to acquit.

TSEDEK: This root of the word means a full weight or measure; from it evolved the word meaning right toward God, or righteousness.

Israel was commanded to walk in the paths of righteousness and to offer the sacrifices of righteousness, putting their trust in the Lord. Jehovah, who is perfectly righteous, cannot overlook the lack of righteousness in man, for "He will by no means clear the guilty" *(Numbers 14:18)*.

It was prophesied by Isaiah that "in the Lord shall all the seed of Israel be justified" *(Isaiah 45:25)*. Jesus is that righteousness for both the Jews and the Gentiles; it is bestowed upon us as a free gift through faith.

JEHOVAH-TSIDKENU reveals to us the method and the measure of our acceptance before God, cleansed in the blood of the Lamb and clothed with the white robe of the righteousness of Him who is Jehovah-Jesus.

JEHOVAH-SHAMMAH:
"Jehovah is there"

The city shall be 18,000 cubits round about; and the name of the city from that day shall be, "The Lord is There."

Ezekiel 48:35

DEFINITION: The Lord is present, the Lord is there; His fullness dwells among us, He tabernacles with us, His glory is manifested among us.

JEHOVAH-SHAMMAH is the promise and pledge of the completion of that purpose in man's final rest and glory. For man's end is to glorify God and enjoy Him forever.

Ezekiel's prophecy of hope and consolation predicts the restoration of the land and people in a measure far beyond anything they had ever experienced in the past, or could have imagined.

The uniqueness of Israel had always been that the presence of God dwelled with them. The condition of His continued presence among them was their faithfulness to a covenant, by which they promised to be a holy people to a holy God.

The fullness of Jehovah's presence is our hope and end of all prophetic expectation, for we are both waiting and longing for His appearing. We are looking for the new heaven and the new earth where His righteousness will dwell with us forever.

JEHOVAH-ROHI:
"Jehovah my shepherd"

The Lord is my shepherd, I shall not want.

Psalm 23:1

DEFINITION: Companion, friend, to cherish, to feed or lead, to guide and direct and instruct.

The title SHEPHERD shows us that God is able to condescend to a relationship with mortal, sinful creatures whom He has redeemed. It suggests a one-on-one relationship to feed us and keep us as His inheritance *(2 Samuel 7:8; Psalm 78:70-72)*.

Shepherding has not changed much in Palestine. A Palestinian shepherd lives with his animals night and day, establishing true intimacy with them. He calls each one by name, and they, knowing his voice and responding only to his call, follow him. By sleeping in the makeshift sheepfold, he protects the sheep from thieves and from preying animals who would devour them at night. The sheep sense his watchfulness and fear no evil. He provides pasture and water for them even in the wilderness.

If there can exist such a tender intimacy between a man and his sheep, how much more so between Jehovah and man, whom He Himself created? What a marvelous thing that God should offer Himself in such a relationship.

This portrays how we are in the shadow of our Father's loving care, watchful protection, and strong defense. He truly keeps us from all evil. He never slumbers nor sleeps. He is attached and devoted to us and protects our lives from perils and pitfalls.

God is an intensely personal Shepherd. He knows each one of us individually.

Jesus is our Good Shepherd who came to gently lead us. He qualified Himself to become the Great

Shepherd by first becoming a lamb, thus entering intimately into every experience and need of a sheep.

DAILY PRAYERS

DAILY PRAYERS

GUIDELINES FOR DAILY USE

This section was originally written for those who intercede for missionaries, ministers and spiritual leaders, and participate in the Intercessors International Prayer Ministry. These prayers do not have to be limited to leaders, but are easily adapted for use for your church, friends or family, as well.

Topics for prayer have been provided for each day of the week. These prayers will meet the needs of those who are beginning their prayer journey, those who feel they need a little extra help, and the experienced intercessor. You may use any or all of these options; use the system that is most comfortable for you.

Each day of the week has a different emphasis. Let's look at Sunday:

1. If prayer is a way of life for you, you might just take the subject "Favor with God" and pray in whatever way the Spirit of the Lord directs you. Or you might want to combine both topic and subtopic, using it as a guideline, such as *Favor with God, Spiritual Revelation, Anointing,* etc.

2. If you do not feel secure and would like some guidance, start with subtopics, such as *Favor with God, Spiritual Revelation, Anointing,* etc., using each step listed underneath.

3.   Whether experienced or inexperienced, you will find the written prayers valuable (which are based on scriptures).   For example, on Sunday you would pray, "Father, I ask that You give to <u>Pastor Paul and Ruth</u> your spirit of wisdom and revelation in the deep, intimate and full knowledge of You, the eyes of their hearts and understanding being enlightened...."   The written prayers are a guide, not a formula.   Allow the Holy Spirit to lead you in the way He desires to pray through you.

As you pray, you may add additional scriptures relating to the daily topics and subtopics.   You may want to note them in your prayer journal, or write them out as they become a part of your scripture praying.

We encourage you to pray the topics each day as we have written.   The Daily Prayers section has been developed for this purpose—to maintain a daily theme so that each intercessor will be in unity and harmony with other pray-ers around the world.   With each of us united and intent on one purpose, we will pull down the strongholds of the enemy, and our leaders will walk in victory.

Remember your work ahead is going to be challenging and constant. Yes, intercession is WORK, BUT IT HAS HEAVENLY REWARDS.

WEEKLY SCHEDULE AND TOPICS FOR DAILY PRAYERS

SUNDAY:

Psalm 90:17
Favor with God

MONDAY:

Acts 2:47
Favor with Man

TUESDAY:

Habakkuk 2:2
Pure Vision

WEDNESDAY:

1 Thessalonians 5:23
Spirit, Soul, Body

THURSDAY:

Psalm 91
Warfare and Protection

FRIDAY:

Matthew 6:33
Priorities

SATURDAY:

Ephesians 5:33-6:4
Family

DAILY PRAYERS

SUNDAY

Favor with God

I. *Favor with God*

Pray:

1. For leaders to walk in the Spirit, pleasing to the Lord.

2. For leaders to serve the Lord with reverent fear, and rejoice with trembling. *(Psalm 2:10,11)*

3. For leaders to be willing to obey God's direction.

4. For leaders to maintain a teachable spirit.

II. *Spiritual Revelation*

Pray:

1. For the Holy Spirit to give personal direction, teaching, vision.

2. For ever-increasing knowledge of God.

3. For revelation of the depths of God and spiritual knowledge of the Word of God.

III. *Anointing*

Pray:

1. For leaders' work to be of good quality—the best.

2. For leaders to have strength to withstand fiery tests.

3. For leaders to have the seven-fold *Spirit of the Lord*; for the Spirit of the Lord, and the spirits of wisdom, understanding, counsel, strength, knowledge and reverent fear of the Lord to rest upon them.

4. For leaders to be strengthened with power in the inner man.

5. For leaders to be sensitive to God's voice— spiritual ears and heart.

6. For leaders to speak the Word with boldness wherever they go.

7. For gifts of the Spirit to flow through leaders: words of wisdom and knowledge, faith, healing, working of miracles, prophecy, distinguishing of spirits, tongues and interpretation of tongues.

8. For leaders to be full of mercy and compassion, walking in forgiveness; enabled to counsel others with God's mercy, grace.

9. For leaders to speak and preach with such an anointing from the Spirit of God that all

unsaved who hear will come to a saving knowledge of Jesus Christ as Lord.

IV. *Holiness*

Pray:

1. Bind all principalities and powers assigned to hinder leaders' place of abiding with God in devotional time.

2. For leaders to set aside ample time for prayer and fellowship with the Lord in productive, personal manner.

3. For leaders to know the depths of God's love; to be grounded in love.

4. For leaders to be sensitive to the Father's heart.

5. For leaders to be good stewards of gifts, talents, time, and money.

6. For leaders to live lives of faith and trust in the Lord.

7. For leaders to let Jesus be glorified in their lives—be good role models.

8. For leaders to walk in holiness in every area of life.

SUNDAY PRAYER

Father, in Jesus' name, I come boldly and with confidence to the throne of grace to obtain mercy and receive grace to help in time of need for (names). *(Hebrews 4:16 KJV/NAS)*

REVELATION
Father, I ask that You give to (names) Your spirit of wisdom and revelation in the deep, intimate, full knowledge of You, the eyes of their hearts and understanding being enlightened and flooded with light, that they might know what is the hope of their calling, and what are the riches of the glory of Your inheritance in them, and what is the exceeding greatness of Your power toward them, because they do believe according to the working of Your mighty power which You wrought in Christ, when You raised Him from the dead, and set Him at Your own right hand in the heavenly places. *(Ephesians 1:17-20 KJV/AMP/Marshall Interlinear/Youngs Literal)*

And Father, even as Your servant Moses was faithful in all Your house, and You spoke to him face to face, even so I pray that (names) will be faithful and entrusted in all Your house, and that You would speak face to face, and mouth to mouth with them—openly, clearly, and directly, and not in dark sayings or riddles. *(Numbers 12:7,8 AMP/NAS/NIV)*

I pray (names) will keep and obey Your commandments and words so that they may continue to abide in Your love, so that You will come unto them and make Your abode and special dwelling place with them, and love them, and show and reveal and manifest Yourself to them, and make Yourself real and be clearly seen by them. *(John 15:9,10 KJV/AMP; John 14:21,23 KJV/AMP)*

ANOINTING

Father, I ask that the Spirit of the Lord rest upon (names)—the spirit of wisdom and understanding, the spirit of counsel and might and strength, the spirit of knowledge and of the reverential and obedient fear of the Lord. *(Isaiah 11:2 AMP/NAS)*

I pray (names) will not be vague or thoughtless or foolish, but will be understanding, firmly grasping the will of the Lord; that they may ever be continually filled with the Holy Spirit, and with the fruit that the Holy Spirit produces: love, joy, peace, patience, kindness, goodness, faithfulness, gentleness, and self-control. I pray that (names) walk and live habitually in the Holy Spirit, responsive to, controlled and guided and led by the Holy Spirit, so that they will not gratify or carry out the cravings and desires of the flesh, and not be subject to, or come under the law. *(Ephesians 5:17,18 AMP; Galatians 5:22,23; Galatians 5:16,18 AMP/NAS)*

Father, grant that the manifestation of the Spirit be given to (names) to profit withal: the word of wisdom, the word of knowledge, faith, gifts of healing, the working of miracles, prophecy, discerning of spirits, kinds of tongues, and the interpretation of tongues. *(1 Corinthians 12:7-10 KJV)*

I pray these attesting signs will accompany (names) because they believe.

In Your name (names) will drive out demons; they will speak in new languages; if they pick up serpents or drink anything deadly, it will not hurt them; (names) will lay their hands on the sick, and they will get well. *(Mark 16:17,18 AMP)*

And, Father, I pray that as (names) go out and preach everywhere, You will keep working with them, and keep confirming the message by the attesting signs and miracles that closely accompany the message. *(Mark 16:20 AMP)*

Father, I pray that (names') speech and their preaching not be set forth in persuasive, enticing and plausible words of man's wisdom, but in demonstration of the Holy Spirit and power, that is a proof by Your Spirit and power operating through them and stirring in the minds of their listeners and hearers, the most holy emotions, and thus, persuading them, so that their faith might not rest in the wisdom of men or in human philosophy, but in the power of God. *(1 Corinthians 2:4,5 AMP/KJV)*

Father, I pray that (names) retain the standard of sound words, in the faith and love which are in Christ Jesus, and that You open up to them a door for the Word, so they may speak forth the mystery of Christ, in order that they may make it clear in the way they ought to speak, and that their speech always be with grace, seasoned with salt, so they may know how to respond to each person. *(2 Timothy 1:13; Colossians 4:3,4,6)*

HOLINESS

And, Father, like the Holy One who called them is holy, I pray that (names) may be holy also in all their behavior. *(1 Peter 1:15,16)*

I ask that (names) may be filled with the knowledge of Your will in all spiritual wisdom and understanding, so that they may walk in a manner worthy of the Lord, to please You in all respects, bearing fruit in every good work and increasing in the knowledge of God, strengthened with all power, according to Your glorious might, for the attaining of all steadfastness and patience. *(Colossians 1:9-11)*

I pray that You will instruct (names) and teach them in the way they should go, and counsel them with Your eye upon them. *(Psalm 32:8)*

FAVOR WITH GOD

I pray that (names) will trust in You, in order that lovingkindness and mercy may surround them. That they will not trust in mankind or make flesh their strength, but trust in the Lord that they may be blessed. *(Psalm 32:10 NAS/KJV; Jeremiah 17:5,7)*

I pray (names) will continue in the faith firmly established, grounded and settled, and steadfast, and not be moved away from the hope of the gospel. *(Colossians 1:23 NAS/KJV)*

I pray they will abide vitally united to You, and that Your words will remain in and continue to live in their hearts, so that (names) may ask whatever they will and it shall be done for them. For You have called and chosen them that they might go and bring forth much fruit, and keep on bearing lasting, remaining, abiding fruit, that You may be honored and glorified, and that (names) may show and prove themselves to be true followers and disciples of Yours. *(John 15:7,16,8 AMP/NAS/KJV)*

I pray, Father, that (names) continue building themselves up on their most holy faith, praying in the Holy Spirit, keeping themselves in the love of God, and looking for the mercy of our Lord Jesus Christ unto eternal life. *(Jude 20,21 KJV)*

Now to Him, who is able to establish (names) according to the gospel and the preaching of Jesus Christ, according to the revelation of the mystery which has been kept secret for long ages past, but now is manifested, and by the Scriptures of the prophets, according to the commandment of the eternal God, which has been made known to all the nations, leading to obedience of faith; now to the only wise God, through Jesus Christ, be the glory forever. Amen. *(Romans 16:25-27)*

MONDAY

Favor With Man

I. *Congregation and All Who Receive Ministry From Leaders*

Pray:

1. That they have teachable spirits and open hearts.

2. That they grow up to be wise and strong.

3. That they be supportive and responsive to leaders with love, prayers, encouragement, finances.

4. That all deluding influences be kept away from them.

5. That they not be followers of "tradition."

6. That they be open to new moves of the Holy Spirit.

7. That they be sensitive to financial needs of the spiritual leaders and ministry, and support them.

8. That gossip, deceit, and unbelief be kept away.

9. That revival spring forth in their lives, church, community, state and nation.

10. That God send His ministering angels to guard them.

II. *Ministry Staff*

Pray:

1. That they be in unity and tuned to the Holy Spirit for direction—be supportive of one another.

2. That they esteem one another more highly than themselves.

3. That they communicate clearly, and not be misunderstood.

4. That no weapon formed against them shall prosper.

5. That they work together well as a team.

6. That they each be honest in their relationships with one another.

7. That they be faithful in commitment to one another and congregation or ministry.

III. *Leaders' Relationship with the Staff*

Pray:

1. That they communicate clearly and not be misunderstood.

2. That they be able to impart the "vision" God has given them to other staff members.

3. That they relate well to each one on an individual basis with much wisdom, understanding and sensitivity.

4. That God give them the needed anointing for their job.

5. That they be peacemakers.

6. That God give them a spirit of wisdom, understanding, knowledge, counsel, strength and obedient and reverent fear of the Lord. *(Isaiah 11:2)*

7. That each one complete the work given him/her to do.

IV. *Unsaved*

Pray:

1. That the leaders witness effectively and boldly to the lost.

2. That God prepare the hearts of those with whom they will share the gospel.

3. That the people they preach or witness to be saved and filled with the Holy Spirit.

4. That Satan not snatch away the Word that has been planted in their hearts.

V. *Government*

Pray:

1. For wisdom and direction for government leaders in the nations.

2. For them to know that they are in the hands of the Lord and He turns them wherever He wishes. *(Proverbs 21:1)*

3. For their hearts to be open to receive the Word of God, salvation in Jesus Christ alone.

4. For laws of their nation to be established on honest biblical principles.

5. For the eyes of their understanding to be opened to truth in God's Word.

6. For revival to sweep through the government offices and no seed planted be stolen.

7. Bind all violence and anti-christ spirits over the government agencies.

8. Bind away the powers of the enemy keeping them from hearing and responding to the gospel. Loose them from false gods, ancestral traditions, and any other influences or spirits that keep them from receiving the full gospel of Jesus Christ.

MONDAY PRAYER

GOVERNMENT

Father, in Jesus' name, I come first of all to pray for leaders and all that are in authority in the countries where (names) live and minister, in order that they may lead a quiet and tranquil and peaceable life in all godliness and dignity and honesty. For this is good and acceptable in Your sight, for You desire all men to be saved and to come to the knowledge of the truth. *(1 Timothy 2:1-4 NAS/KJV)*

I pray, Father, that these rulers in authority in (name of country) be not a terror to good works, but to the evil; that these rulers be Your ministers and revengers to execute wrath upon them that do evil. *(Romans 13:3 KJV)*

Give these leaders knowledge of Your way of judging, O God, and give them the Spirit of Your righteousness to control all their actions. Let them judge and govern Your people with righteousness, and Your poor and afflicted with judgment and justice. I pray the mountains bring peace to the people, and the hills, through the general establishment of righteousness. May these leaders judge and defend the poor of the people, deliver the children of the needy, and crush the oppressor so that all may revere and fear You while the sun and moon endure, throughout all generations. *(Psalm 72:1-5 AMP)*

I pray these leaders in authority will deliver the needy when he calls, the poor also and him who has no helper; that the leaders will have pity on the poor and weak and needy, and that they will save the lives of the needy, and redeem their lives from oppression and fraud and violence, and that precious and costly shall be the blood of the needy in Your sight and in the sight of the leaders. *(Psalm 72:12-14 AMP)*

I pray that prayer shall be made for the needy continually, and that men shall be blessed by these leaders and that all nations shall call them and You blessed. *(Psalm 72:15,17 AMP)*

Father, I pray that You take away the wicked from before these leaders in authority in (name of country) so their government will be established in righteousness. For promotion comes not from the east, nor from the west, nor from the south, but You are judge. You put down one and lift up another. I pray they may be surrounded with many wise and righteous counselors who love peace. *(Proverbs 25:5; Psalm 75:6,7 AMP/NAS; Proverbs 12:20)*

I pray, Father, that these leaders in authority will not desire strong drink nor wine, lest they drink and forget the law, and pervert the judgment of any of the afflicted. I pray they will not receive a bribe from the bosom to pervert the ways of justice, but that they will give stability to the land by justice, and not take a bribe to overthrow it. *(Proverbs 31:4,5 KJV/NAS; Proverbs 17:23; Proverbs 29:4)*

Lord, counsel is Yours, and sound wisdom. You are understanding, and power is Yours. By You kings reign, and rulers decree justice. By You princes rule, and nobles, and all who judge rightly. I pray these rulers in authority will diligently seek You so that they may find You. *(Proverbs 8:14-17)*

THOSE NOT SAVED

Father, having overlooked the times of ignorance, You are now declaring to men that all men everywhere should repent, because You have fixed a day in which You will judge the world in righteousness, through Jesus Christ whom You have appointed, having furnished proof to all men by raising Him from the dead. *(Acts 17:30,31)*

Father, You are not slow about Your promise, as some count slowness, but You are patient toward us, not wishing for any to perish, but for all to come to repentance. For the Son of Man has come to seek, and to save that which was lost, and You said, "I will have mercy, and not sacrifice: For I am not come to call the righteous, but sinners to repentance." *(2 Peter 3:9; Luke 19:10; Matthew 9:13 KJV)*

Lord, according to Your Word, I am asking for the heathen for (names') inheritance, and the uttermost parts of the earth for their possession. *(Psalm 2:8 KJV)*

Father, I ask that You grant sinners, who will be ministered to by (names), repentance from dead works, and faith toward God. That these sinners put aside all filthiness and all that remains of wickedness. And I pray that they receive in humility the engrafted Word, which is able to save their souls. *(Hebrews 6:1 KJV; James 1:21 NAS/KJV)*

I ask that You pour out on sinners, who will be ministered to by (names), Your Spirit of grace and supplication so that they can look on Jesus, whom they have pierced. I ask that Your Spirit of truth come and convict them concerning sin, righteousness and judgment; convict sinners concerning sin because they do not believe in Jesus; convict sinners concerning righteousness because Jesus went back to You; and convict sinners concerning judgment because the ruler of this world has been judged. *(Zechariah 12:10; John 16:8-11,13)*

Thank You, Father, You are able to save forever those who draw near to You through Jesus, since He always lives to make intercession for them. I pray these sinners receive Your Spirit of adoption

as sons, by which they may cry out, "ABBA! Father!"
I pray the Holy Spirit, Himself, will bear witness with
their spirit, and that they become the children of God.
(Hebrews 7:25; Romans 8:15,16)

THOSE NEEDING MINISTRY
I pray, Father, that You open a door for the Word,
so (names) may speak forth the mystery of Christ; and
that they may make it clear in the way they ought to
speak. *(Colossians 4:3,4)*

I pray (names) would conduct themselves with
wisdom toward outsiders, making the most of their
opportunities and using their time wisely. I pray their
speech be always with grace, seasoned, as it were, with
salt, so that they may know how to respond to each
person. *(Colossians 4:5,6)*

I pray, Father, that those receiving ministry
continue in the faith firmly established and steadfast,
grounded and settled, and that they not be moved away
from the hope of the gospel which they have heard.
Sanctify them in Your truth; Your Word is truth.
(Colossians 1:23 NAS/KJV; John 17:17)

May the Word of the Lord spread rapidly and be
glorified. May (names), as well as those receiving
ministry, be delivered from perverse and evil men, for
not all have faith. Thank you, Father, that because You
are faithful, You will strengthen them and protect them
from the evil one. *(2 Thessalonians 3:1-3)*

I pray that the hearts of those receiving ministry
may be comforted and encouraged, being knit together
in love, and attaining to all the wealth which comes
from the full assurance of understanding, resulting in a
true knowledge of Your mystery, that is Christ
Himself, in whom are hidden all the treasures of
wisdom and knowledge. *(Colossians 2:2,3 NAS;KJV)*

LEADERSHIP AND STAFF

Holy Father, I thank You that no weapon formed against (names) or their co-workers, or their families, or their ministries, shall prosper, and every tongue that has risen against them in judgment shall be shown to be in the wrong. For this peace, righteousness, security, and triumph over opposition is the heritage of these servants of the Lord, and this is the righteousness and vindication which they obtain from You—that which You impart to them as their justification. *(Isaiah 54:17 AMP)*

Since then, Father, (names) have been raised up with Christ to a new life, thus sharing Jesus' resurrection from the dead, I pray that they aim at and keep seeking the rich, eternal treasures that are above, where Christ is, seated at the right hand of God. That they set their minds and keep them set on what is above, the higher things, not on the things that are on the earth. For as far as this world is concerned, they have died and their new real life is hid with Christ in God. *(Colossians 3:1-3 AMP/NAS)*

I pray that (names) be of the same mind, maintaining the same love, united in spirit, intent on one purpose. That they walk in a manner worthy of the calling with which they have been called, with all humility and gentleness, with patience, showing forbearance to one another in love, being diligent to preserve the unity of the Spirit in the bond of peace and forgiving one another, whoever has a complaint against any one, just as the Lord forgave them. May they give no cause for offense in anything, in order that the ministry be not discredited, but in everything commending themselves as servants of God. *(Philippians 2:2; Ephesians 4:1-3; Colossians 3:13 NAS/KJV; 2 Corinthians 6:3,4)*

I pray that whatever these staff members do,

they do their work heartily as for the Lord rather than for men, knowing that from the Lord they will receive the reward of the inheritance; for it is the Lord Christ whom they serve. *(Colossians 3:23,24)*

FAVOR

For You, Lord, will bless the righteous. As with a shield You will surround (names) with good will, pleasure and favor. *(Psalm 5:12 AMP)*

Father, I pray Your servants will not forsake mercy and kindness and truth, but that they will shut out all hatred and selfishness and deliberate hypocrisy and falsehood. I pray (names) will bind mercy and kindness and truth about their necks, and write them on the tablet of their hearts, so that they may find favor, good understanding and high esteem in the sight and judgment of God and man. *(Proverbs 3:3,4 AMP)*

Father, I pray that in all matters of wisdom and understanding, when (names) are consulted, that their counsel will be found to be ten times better than the counsel of all those in the whole country round about. *(Daniel 1:20 KJV/NAS/AMP)*

TUESDAY

Pure Vision

I. *Vision*

Pray:

1. For God to clarify His vision for ministry to these leaders.

2. For patience until its fulfillment.

3. For finances for the vision to come forth.

4. For a "wall of fire" to protect the vision. *(Zechariah 2:5)*

5. For helpers in carrying out the vision.

6. Do spiritual warfare against tactics of the enemy that would delay vision from coming forth in God's timing.

7. Stop the mouths of those who would speak against the vision.

II. *Wisdom and Enlightenment*

Pray:

1. For the Holy Spirit to continually give enlightenment and reveal hidden knowledge of the mysteries of Christ.

2. For keen discernment between God's wisdom and human wisdom.

3. For a teachable spirit.

4. For them to not depend on past experience or direction, but seek fresh wisdom and guidance before making any decision.

III. *Motives*

Pray:

1. For pure motives, purged by God through the Word and prayer time.

2. For awareness that God can give right motives.

3. For God to continually renew thought life and a right spirit within.

4. For any wrong motives/thoughts done in darkness to be brought to light, and dealt with in a Christ-like way.

5. For discernment against impure motives; for wisdom and knowledge on how to deal with them, and the discipline to do it.

IV. *Guidance*

Pray:

1. For dependence on God for guidance during prayer time and all during the day as decisions are made.

2.   For right people to come into their life at the right time to give godly counsel.

3.   For God to lead and direct their paths.

TUESDAY PRAYER

UNDERSTANDING

Father, In Jesus' name, I come before You making request with intercession for (names). Father, I thank You for these precious "lovegifts" to the Body of Christ. *(Ephesians 1:16 and 4:8)*

Thank You, Father, that the Son of God has come, and has given (names) understanding, in order that they might know Him who is true. *(1 John 5:20)*

Thank You, Father, that wisdom is in the presence of the one who has understanding, and that because (names) seek You, they can understand all things. For You give wisdom, and out of Your mouth comes knowledge and understanding. *(Proverbs 17:24; Proverbs 28:5; Proverbs 2:6 KJV)*

I pray they may be of quick understanding, and that their delight be in the reverential and obedient fear of the Lord.   May (names) not judge by what their eyes see, nor make a decision by what their ears hear; but with righteousness may they judge the poor, and decide with fairness for the afflicted of the earth.   May they smite the earth and the oppressor with the rod of their mouths, and with the breath of their lips slay the wicked. May righteousness be the belt around their loins, and faithfulness the belt around their waists. *(Isaiah 11:3-5 AMP/NAS)*

WISDOM

Thank You, Father, (names) have an anointing from the Holy One, and they know all things. *(1 John 2:20 NAS/KJV)*

Thank You, Father, that by Your doing they are in Christ Jesus, who became to them wisdom from God, righteousness, sanctification, and redemption. *(1 Corinthians 1:30)*

I pray, Father, that (names) will be wise and understanding, and show by their good behavior their deeds in the gentleness of wisdom that is from above: being first pure, then peaceable, gentle, reasonable, full of mercy and good fruits, unwavering, and without hyprocrisy. And that the fruit of righteousness be sown in peace by (names), who make peace. *(James 3:13,17,18 NAS/KJV)*

I pray that wisdom and knowledge shall be the stability of their times and strength of salvation; and that the fear of the Lord is their treasure. *(Isaiah 33:6 KJV)*

GUIDANCE

I pray (names) will trust in You, Lord, with all their hearts; and that they will not lean on their own understanding. I pray that in all their ways they will acknowledge You, and You will make their paths straight. For You, Father, lead the humble in justice, and teach the humble Your way. *(Proverbs 3:5,6; Psalm 25:9)*

A man's way is not in himself; nor is it in a man who walks to direct his steps. The steps of (names) are ordered by You, Father, and You delight in their way. *(Psalm 37:23 KJV; Jeremiah 10:23)*

Make them to know Your ways, Father; teach them Your paths. Lead them in Your truth and teach them, for You are the God of their salvation; for You they wait all the day. *(Psalm 25:4,5)*

Thank You, Father, for You teach (names) to profit, and lead them in the way they should go. *(Isaiah 48:17)*

ENLIGHTENMENT

Lord of Glory, I pray that You might give to (names) Your spirit of wisdom and revelation in the sphere of a full knowledge of Yourself, with the eyes of their hearts being in an enlightened state with a view to their knowing what is the hope of Your calling, and what is the wealth of the glory of Your inheritance in them as saints, and what is the superabounding greatness of Your inherent power to them who are the believing ones, as measured by the operative energy of the manifested strength of Your might. *(Ephesians 1:17-19 Wuest)*

And, Father, I pray that You would make known to (names) the mystery of Your will according to Your good pleasure which You have purposed in Yourself. *(Ephesians 1:9 KJV)*

WILL OF GOD AND VISION

Father, I ask that You fill Your servants with a clear knowledge of Your will by giving them every kind of spiritual wisdom and understanding, so they might live worthy of the Lord, aiming to please You in every way as they produce every kind of good work, and grow by knowing You better. *(Colossians 1:9,10 Beck)*

Father, I pray that You would count (names) worthy of this calling, and that they would fulfill every good pleasure of Your goodness, and the work of faith with power, in order that the name of our Lord Jesus may be glorified in them, and they in Him, according to the grace of our God and the Lord Jesus Christ. *(2 Thessalonians 1:11,12 Marshall Interlinear/KJV)*

I pray (names) will intimately come to know and recognize, and listen to and heed, the voice of the Good Shepherd. For You call them by name and lead them out. I pray they follow You, because they know Your voice; that they will never on any account follow a stranger, but will run away from him, because they do not know the voice of strangers or recognize their call. *(John 10:3-5 AMP)*

MINISTRY

Precious Father, I pray that (names) might fully carry out the preaching of the Word of God; that is, the mystery which has been hidden from the past ages and generations; but which has now been manifested to Your saints, to whom You willed to make known what are the riches of the glory of this mystery among the Gentiles, which is Christ in them, the hope of glory. *(Colossians 1:25b-27)*

And, Father, I pray that (names) will proclaim Christ, admonishing and teaching every man with all wisdom, that they may present every man complete in Christ, striving according to Your power, which mightily works within them. *(Colossians 1:28,29)*

I ask that You give them utterance and wisdom which none of their opponents will be able to resist or refute. *(Luke 21:15)*

THOUGHTS, MOTIVES, RENEWED MIND

Father, I pray (names) be not conformed to this world, but that they be transformed by the renewing of their minds, that they may prove what Your will is, that which is good and acceptable and perfect. That they pull down every stronghold, cast down every imagination and every high thing that exalts itself against the knowledge of God, and bring into captivity every thought to the obedience of Christ. *(Romans 12:2; 2 Corinthians 10:4,5 KJV)*

Father, whatever is true, whatever is honorable, whatever is right, whatever is pure, whatever is lovely, whatever is of good repute, if there is any excellence and if anything worthy of praise, may (names) let their mind dwell on these things. *(Philippians 4:8)*

Create in them a clean heart, Holy Father, and renew a steadfast spirit within them. Do not cast (names) away from Your presence, and do not take Your Holy Spirit from them. Restore to them the joy of Your salvation, and sustain them with a willing spirit. Then will they teach transgressors Your ways, and sinners will be converted to You. *(Psalm 51:10-13)*

DAILY PRAYERS

WEDNESDAY

Spirit, Soul, Body

I. *Health*

Pray:

1. For divine health—physically, mentally, emotionally.

2. For all effects of tiredness and discouragement to be loosed from their bodies and minds.

3. For the leaders to recognize need to care for their physical bodies with adequate rest.

4. For wisdom and self-control in eating (loosed from compulsion).

5. For time to exercise properly.

6. For adequate strength to accomplish tasks.

II. *Appearance*

Pray:

1. For leaders to maintain the glow of Jesus.

2. For leaders to attract others to the Lord through tidy appearance, right actions, gentle speech.

III. *Attitudes*

Pray:

1. For fruits of the Spirit. *(Galatians 5:22,23)*

2. For gracious but firm attitude—learn when/how to say "no."

3. For mercy, compassion.

4. For desire to be a peacemaker and to restore broken relationships.

5. For total submission to the Lord in every area of life.

6. For a spirit of unity, not competition.

7. For humility rather than superiority.

8. For cooperation rather than defensiveness.

9. For discernment to recognize wrong attitudes in themselves, and courage to deal with them immediately.

IV. *Spiritual and Physical Wholeness*

Pray:

1. For leaders to pursue righteousness, faith, love and peace.

2. For leaders to refuse foolish and ignorant speculations.

3. For leaders to have a desire to go on with Jesus regardless of the cost involved.

4. For leaders to feed daily on the Word of God, meditating on God's precepts.

5. For leaders to commune with God daily in prayer.

WEDNESDAY PRAYER

HEALTH

Thank You, Father, through Jesus Christ for (names); in Jesus' name I bring these requests and petitions before You in their behalf.

Thank You for sending Your Word, the Lord Jesus, and healing (names) and delivering them from their destructions. I give You thanks for Your lovingkindness, and for Your wonders to the sons of men. I pray they will also offer You sacrifices of thanksgiving, and tell of Your works with joyful singing. *(Psalm 107:20-22)*

Father, I pray that (names) give attention to Your words, and incline their ears to Your sayings; that they do not let them depart from their sight, and that they keep them in the midst of their hearts, because they are life to those who find them and health to their whole body. *(Proverbs 4:20-22)*

Thank You, Father, that because (names) serve You, You will bless their bread and their water, and You will remove sickness from their midst. *(Exodus 23:25)*

Father, I pray their souls bless You, and that they not forget any of Your benefits: for You pardon all their iniquities; You heal all their diseases; You redeem their lives from the pit; You crown (names) with lovingkindness and compassion; You satisfy their years and desires with good things so that their youth is renewed like the eagle's; and You, only, perform righteous deeds, and judgments for all who are oppressed. *(Psalm 103:2-6)*

Father, thank You that the Spirit of Him who raised Jesus from the dead dwells in (names), and that because You raised Christ Jesus from the dead, You will also give life to their mortal bodies through Your Spirit who indwells them. *(Romans 8:11)*

I thank You, Father, that Jesus, Himself, bore their sins in His own body on the cross, that they might die to sin and live to righteousness; for by His wounds they were healed. *(1 Peter 2:24)*

Thank You, Father, that Christ has redeemed (names) from the curse of the Law, having become a curse for them, for it is written, "Cursed is every one who hangs on a tree," in order that in Christ Jesus the blessing of Abraham might come to the Gentiles, that they might receive the promise of the Spirit through faith. Thank You, Father, (names) belong to Christ, and are Abraham's offspring, and heirs according to promise. *(Galatians 3:13,14,29)*

APPEARANCE

O, Father, Christ gave Himself up for (names), that He might sanctify and cleanse them with the washing of water by the Word, that He might present them to Himself, not having spot or wrinkle, or any such thing, but that they should be holy and without blemish. *(Ephesians 5:25b-27 KJV)*

I pray, Father, that whatever (names) do in word or deed, they do it all in the name of the Lord Jesus, giving thanks through Him to You. *(Colossians 3:17)*

Thank You, Father, (names) have put on righteousness, and it clothes them; their justice is like a robe and a turban. *(Job 29:14)*

I pray they be clothed with strength and dignity. I pray they also clothe themselves with humility toward one another, for You are opposed to the proud, but give grace to the humble. I pray (names) will humble themselves, therefore, under Your mighty hand, that You may exalt them at the proper time; that they cast all their anxiety upon You, because You care for them. *(Proverbs 31:25a; 1 Peter 5:5b-7)*

I pray, Father, that no one look down on (names), but rather in speech, conduct, love, faith and purity, they will show themselves an example of those who believe. *(1 Timothy 4:12)*

Father, I pray (names) will abstain from all appearance of evil. *(1 Thessalonians 5:22 KJV)*

SPIRITUAL AND PHYSICAL WHOLENESS

I pray, Father, that (names) discipline themselves for the purpose of godliness; for bodily discipline is only of little profit, but godliness is profitable for all things, since it holds promise for the present life and also for the life to come. *(1 Timothy 4:7,8)*

I pray (names) will glorify God in their bodies, for they have been bought with a price, and are not their own; for their bodies are a temple for the Holy Spirit. *(1 Corinthians 6:19,20)*

I pray they will not hurt or destroy the temple of God, for the temple of God is holy, and that is what they are. *(1 Corinthians 3:16,17)*

Thank you, Father, that (names) are a building being fitted together and growing into a holy temple in the Lord, in whom they also are being built together into a dwelling of God in the Spirit. *(Ephesians 2:21,22)*

I pray, Father, that (names) cleanse themselves from wickedness, that they will be vessels for honor, sanctified and useful to You, prepared for every good work. I pray that they flee from youthful lusts, and pursue righteousness, faith, love and peace with those who call on the Lord from a pure heart. And that they refuse foolish and ignorant speculations, knowing they produce quarrels. *(2 Timothy 2:21-23)*

ATTITUDE

Thank You, Father, (names) have been called to freedom; only I pray they do not turn their freedom into an opportunity for the flesh, but through love may they serve one another. For the whole law is fulfilled in one word, in the statement, "You shall love your neighbor as yourself." *(Galatians 5:13,14)*

I pray, Father, that (names) forget what lies behind and reach forward to what lies ahead, pressing on toward the goal for the prize of the upward call of God in Christ Jesus. And if in anything they have a different attitude, Father, I pray You reveal it also to them. *(Philippians 3:13-15)*

So, Father, I pray (names) do nothing from selfishness or empty conceit, but with humility of mind let them each regard one another as more important than themselves; that they do not merely look out for their own personal interests, but also for the interests of others. I pray they will have the same attitude in themselves which was also in Christ Jesus. *(Philippians 2:3-5)*

BLESSINGS

Father, I pray that You bless (names), and keep them; that You make Your face to shine on them, and be gracious to them; that You lift up Your countenance upon them, and give them peace. *(Numbers 6:24-26)*

Cause (names) to increase and abound in love for one another, and for all men, so that You may establish their hearts unblamable in holiness before You at the coming of our Lord Jesus with all Your saints. *(1 Thessalonians 3:12,13)*

Father, I pray (names) will fear You and keep Your commandments, for this is the whole duty of man and what You require of them for their good: that they fear You; that they walk in all Your ways; that they love You, and serve You out of and with their whole hearts, and with all their souls, and with all their minds, their faculties of thought, of quick apprehension, intelligence, keenness of discernment, and moral understanding, and with all their strength. *(Mark 12:30,33 AMP/NAS; Eccl. 12:13 KJV; Deuteronomy 10:12,13 AMP/NAS)*

DAILY PRAYERS

THURSDAY

Warfare and Protection

I. *Protection*

Pray:

1. That God send angels to guard over
    missionaries, ministers, spiritual leaders, their
    families, and property—make a hedge to
    guard all that is going in and coming out, the
    air above and the ground below.

2. That the angels go before them and do battle
    in the leaders' behalf. (Example: Michael, one
    of the chief princes, doing battle on Daniel's
    behalf.) *(Daniel 10:13)*

3. That God foil all attacks and traps of the
    enemy and keep the leaders from the nets of
    the enemy while they walk by safely. *(Psalms
    35; 37; 141:9,10)*

4. That God be the leaders' hiding place and
    preserve them from trouble, surrounding them
    with songs of deliverance. *(Psalm 32:7)*

5. For the leaders' protection. *(Psalm 91)*

6. That the Holy Spirit open the leaders' eyes to the plans, plots, ploys and traps of the enemy.

7. That the Holy Spirit go before them and make the crooked places straight and shatter the doors of bronze and cut through the bars of iron. *(Isaiah 45:2)*

II. *Temptation*

Pray:

1. That the missionaries, ministers, and spiritual leaders stand firm and not succumb to the difficult times of the last days—that they not be lovers of self, lovers of money, boastful, proud, abusive, disobedient to parents, ungrateful, unholy, without love, unforgiving, slanderous, without self-control, brutal, not lovers of good, treacherous, rash, conceited, lovers of pleasure rather than lovers of God. (See *2 Timothy 3:2-4.*)

2. That the leaders not fall to the lust of the flesh, the lust of the eyes, nor the pride of life. *(1 John 2:16)*

3. That they walk humbly before their God.

4. That the leaders stand firm in the Word of God.

III. *Deception*

Pray:

1. That the leaders not be led astray nor into error by false doctrine(s) and false prophets. *(Matthew 24:24)*

2. That they not be enamored by signs and wonders from the enemy.

3. That the leaders be kept from error and know the truth so it will keep them free. *(John 8:32)*

4. That the leaders hide the Word in their hearts.

5. That they not walk in hypocrisy or be bound by religious spirits.

6. That they pursue the love of truth.

7. That the leaders not be deceived by an antichrist, antichurch or unholy spirit that operates in signs and wonders.

IV. *Enemies*

Pray:

1. Against principalities, powers, rulers of darkness, and spiritual wickedness in high places that come against the leaders, their families, ministries, and the nations they are in. *(Ephesians 6:12)*

2. Against occult activity—curses, witchcraft, divination, sorcery—in this manner:

a. Bind the strongman. *(Psalm 149; Matthew 12:29; 16:19)*

b. Destroy the works of the enemy. (See prayer in The Name of Jesus section.) For this purpose, Jesus was manifested. *(1 John 3:8)*

c. Ask God to foil the signs of the false prophets and make fools of the diviners. *(Isaiah 44:25)*

d. Send back double the deeds of destruction as they were sent to the leaders, their families, and their properties. *(Revelation 18:6)*

e. Ask that the enemies fall into their own traps while the leaders walk by safely. *(Psalm 141:9,10)*

f. Ask the Lord to avenge His people. *(Psalms 35; 37)*

g. Ask for God's most perfect will to be accomplished in the leaders.

h. Ask God to restore that which the enemy tried to steal, kill and destroy.

i. Ask that the Holy Spirit fill the leaders with the fruits of the Spirit and minister restoration. *(Isaiah 61; Matthew 12:43-45; Galatians 5:22)*

Definitions:

Occult - Literally "hidden." Hidden from the eyes or understanding; invisible; secret; unknown; undiscovered; undetected.

Curse - To utter a wish of evil against one; to invoke evil upon; to call for mischief or injury to fall upon; to execrate; to injure; to subject to evil; to vex, harrass or torment with great calamities.

Witchcraft - The practice of witches; sorcery; enchantment; unnatural power; intercourse with the devil.

Divination - The act of divining; foretelling future events, or discovering things secret or obscure by the aid of superior beings, or by other than human means.

Sorcery - Magic; enchantment; witchcraft; divination by assistance or supposed assistance of evil spirits, or the power of commanding evil spirits.

THURSDAY PRAYER

SAFETY, PROTECTION, RELEASE
FROM FEAR

Father, I come before You in the Name of Jesus, our Great High Priest who is touched with the feeling of our infirmities. Father, I'm interceding for (names). Thank You for hearing and answering my prayer. *(Hebrews 4:15 KJV)*

The Lord lives, and blessed be their rock. And exalted be the God of salvation, for You execute vengeance for them, and subdue peoples under them. You deliver (names) from their enemies; surely You lift them above those who rise up against them; You rescue them from the violent man. Therefore, they will give thanks to You among the nations, O Lord, and will sing praises to Your name. For You give great deliverance to them, and show loving kindness to Your anointed, and their descendants forever. *(Psalm 18:46-50)*

Father, because (names) listen to You and Your wisdom, they shall live securely, and shall be at ease from the dread of evil. Because they have made the Lord their refuge, even the Most High their dwelling place, no evil will befall them, nor will any plague come near their tent. *(Proverbs 1:33; Psalm 91:9,10)*

Father, I pray for (names) to take up the full armor of God that they may be able to resist in the evil day, and that they, having done everything, may stand firm, having girded their loins with truth, and having put on the breastplate of righteousness, and having shod their feet with the preparation of the gospel of peace. In addition to all, may they take up the shield of faith with which they will be able to extinguish all the flaming missiles of the evil one, and taking the helmet of salvation, and the sword of the Spirit, which is the Word of God, with all prayer and petition, may they pray at all times in the Spirit, and with this in view, be on the alert with all perseverance and petition for all the saints. *(Ephesians 6:13-18)*

Thank You, Lord, that in righteousness (names) will be established; they will be far from oppression, for they will not fear; and from terror, for it will not come near them. And if anyone fiercely assails them it will not be from You, for whoever assails them will fall because of them. Father, You declared that no weapon formed against them shall prosper, and every tongue that accuses them in judgment they will condemn. For this is the heritage of Your servants, and their vindication is from You. *(Isaiah 54:14,15,17)*

For You did not give (names) a spirit of timidity, but You have given them a spirit of power and of love and of a calm and well-balanced mind and discipline and self-control. *(2 Timothy 1:7 AMP)*

I pray, Father, that (names) will be strong and courageous, that they not tremble or be dismayed, for You are with them wherever they go. For greater is He who is in them than he who is in the world. *(Joshua 1:9; 1 John 4:4)*

Thank, You, Father, that the angel of the Lord encamps around (names) because they fear You, and he rescues them. You are their confidence, and will keep their feet from being caught. *(Psalm 34:7; Proverbs 3:26)*

Thank You, Father, that You have given them authority through Jesus to tread upon serpents and scorpions, and over all the power of the enemy, and nothing shall injure them. *(Luke 10:19)*

ENEMIES

O, Father, keep (names) as the apple of Your eye; hide them in the shadow of Your wings, from the wicked who despoil them, from their deadly enemies, who surround them. *(Psalm 17:8,9)*

Father, contend with those who contend with (names); fight against those who fight against them. For their eyes are toward You, O God, the Lord; in You they take refuge; do not leave them defenseless. Keep them from the jaws of the traps which have been set for them, and from the snares of those who do iniquity. Let the wicked fall into their own nets, while (names) pass by safely. *(Psalms 35:1; 141:8-10)*

TEMPTATION

Father, I ask that You not lead Your servants into temptation, but deliver them from evil. *(Matthew 6:13)*

I thank You, Father, that no temptation has overtaken (names) but such as is common to man; for You are faithful, and will not allow them to be tempted beyond what they are able, but with the temptation, You will provide the way of escape also, that they may be able to endure it. *(1 Corinthians 10:13)*

Thank You, Father, that You give greater grace. Therefore, it says, "God is opposed to the proud, but gives grace to the humble." I pray, Father, that (names) submit to You, that they may resist the devil and he will flee from them. I pray they will draw near to You, and You will draw near to them. I pray that (names) cleanse their hands, and purify their hearts, in order that they be not double-minded. *(James 4:6-8)*

Father, since Jesus, Himself, was tempted in that which He suffered, He is able to come to the aid of those who are tempted. Since we do not have a High Priest who cannot sympathize with our weaknesses— but one who was tempted in all things as we are, yet without sin—I pray that (names) will therefore draw near with confidence to the throne of grace, that they may receive mercy and find grace to help in time of need. *(Hebrews 4:14-16)*

DECEPTION

I pray, Father, that (names) will beware of the

false prophets, who come to them in sheep's clothing, but inwardly are ravenous wolves. I pray (names) will know and recognize them by their fruits. For every good tree bears good fruit, but the rotten tree bears bad fruit. *(Matthew 7:15-17)*

Father, may (names) see to it that no one misleads them, for Jesus said that many will come in His name, saying, "I am the Christ," and will mislead many. For false Christs and false prophets will arise and will show great signs and wonders, so as to mislead, if possible, even the elect. *(Matthew 24:4,5,24)*

Father, I pray (names) will not believe every spirit, but will test the spirits to see whether they are from You, because many false prophets have gone out into the world. By this they will know the Spirit of God: every spirit that confesses that Jesus Christ has come in the flesh is from God; and every spirit that does not confess Jesus is not from God; and this is the spirit of the antichrist, of which we have heard that it is coming, and now it is already in the world. *(1 John 4:1-3)*

I pray, Father, that (names) not be taken captive through philosophy and empty deception, according to the tradition of men, according to the elementary principles of the world, rather than according to Christ. For in Him they have been made complete, and He (Christ) is the overall rule and authority. *(Colossians 2:8)*

OVERCOMING POWERS OF DARKNESS

Thank You, Father, You have given to us the keys to the kingdom of heaven, and whatever we bind on earth, shall be bound in heaven, and whatever we loose on earth shall be loosed in heaven. *(Matthews 16:19 KJV)*

Father, in Jesus' name, I bind and break off of

(names) and their families and ministries and all things that concern them: all principalities, powers, rulers of darkness of this world, and spiritual wickedness in high places, all occult activity—curses, witchcraft, divination and sorcery. I destroy the works of the enemy over them, and come against any soul power or emotional ties that do not glorify You.

Father, I ask that You forgive (names) for the sins of their youth, all vows, judgments, agreements with lies, and the sins and iniquities of their fathers, back through all generations, including all idle, negative words and curses over them in Jesus' name.

I loose (names) and their families and those with them in the ministry, and all things that concern them into the glorious liberty of the children of God, in the precious name of Jesus. If therefore the Son shall make them free, they shall be free indeed.

(Study references: *Genesis 26:28; Exodus 20:5,6; 34:7,15; Numbers 30:2; Deuteronomy 5:9,10; 23:21; 24:16; Psalm 25:7; Proverbs 6:16-19; 12:13,14; 13:2,3; Ecclesiastes 5:4-7; Isaiah 28:15,18 KJV; Jeremiah 31:19; 32:18; Daniel 9:4-20; Hosea 10:4; Luke 6:37,38 AMP; John 8:36; Romans 2:1-6; Ephesians 6:12,17; 2 Thessalonians 2:10-12 AMP; Hebrews 3:19; 4:11; James 4:11,12; 1 John 1:7,9)*

Thank You, Father, (names) have overcome the enemy because of the blood of the Lamb, and because of the word of their testimony, and they do not love their lives even to death. *(Revelation 12:11)*

Thank You, Father, that (names) have redemption through Jesus' blood, the forgiveness of their trespasses, according to the riches of Your grace. *(Ephesians 1:7)*

Thank You, Father, as the redeemed of the Lord, (names) say so, whom Jesus has redeemed from the hand of the adversary. *(Psalm 107:2)*

Much more, then, having now been justified by Jesus' blood, (names) shall be saved from wrath through Him. For if while they were enemies they were reconciled to You through the death of Your Son, Jesus, much more, having been reconciled, they shall be saved by His life. *(Romans 5:9,10)*

Thank You Father, that You made Jesus, who knew no sin to be sin on (names') behalf, that they might become the righteousness of God in Him. Therefore, Jesus also, that He might sanctify them through His own blood, suffered outside the gate. *(2 Corinthians 5:21; Hebrews 13:12)*

I pray, Father, that there be no strange god among (names), and that they not worship any foreign god. I pray they will not be bound together with unbelievers; for what partnership have righteousness and lawlessness, or what fellowship has light with darkness. *(Psalm 81:9; 2 Corinthians 6:14)*

Thank You, Father, that (names) are a temple of God, and the Spirit of God dwells in them. *(1 Corinthians 3:16)*

DAILY PRAYERS

FRIDAY

Priorities

I. *Finances*

Pray:

1. The Lord will cause the leaders to abound in prosperity—body, soul and spirit.

2. Thank Him for providing for all needs:

   a. Personal
   b. Family
   c. Ministry

3. Ask Him to stir up supporters for the ministry who will be obedient in giving; bless/prosper them for their giving.

4. For the ministry to have favor in eyes of supporters.

5. Thank God that He will rebuke the devourer when he comes to steal what rightly belongs to the ministry of the leaders you pray for.

II. *Priorities*

Pray:

1. For discernment to get priorities in order.

2. For leaders to be open to God's changes and adjustments.

3. For leaders to learn to be wise stewards of time; become disciplined.

4. For leaders' relationship with God to always remain top priority.

III. *Blessings*

Pray:

1. Ask God to bless them because they give tithes and offerings and are cheerful givers.

2. Thank God that His Word says He delights to bless His servants; ask Him to bless the leaders you pray for.

3. Thank God for continuing to bless your leaders even into old age as they serve in His Kingdom.

FRIDAY PRAYER

FINANCES

Father, in Jesus name, I pray for (names). I praise You for Your faithfulness to Your Word. Father, I pray that Your Word will be breathed upon by Your Holy Spirit, in order that it will accomplish the purposes of Your heart that You've sent it to do.

O, Father, You love (names) who love You, and I pray they will diligently seek You in order to find You. For riches and honor are with You, enduring wealth and righteousness. *(Proverbs 8:17,18)*

Father, You cause those that love You to inherit substance, and You will fill their treasuries. *(Proverbs 8:21 KJV)*

Thank You, Father, because the Lord is (names') Shepherd; they shall not want. And thank You, Father, because of the grace of our Lord Jesus Christ, that even though He was rich, yet for their sakes, He became poor, that they through His poverty might become rich. *(Psalm 23:1; 2 Corinthians 8:9)*

Father, I pray (names) will have pity on the poor, for they that have pity on the poor lend to You, and that which they have given will You pay them again. *(Proverbs 19:17 KJV)*

Father, I pray that as (names) give, it will be given to them; good measure, pressed down, shaken together, running over, it will pour into their laps. For whatever measure they deal out to others, it will be dealt to them in return. *(Luke 6:38)*

So, Father, I pray they sow bountifully in order to reap bountifully. May they give as they have purposed in their hearts, not grudgingly or under compulsion, for You love a cheerful giver. And You are able to make all grace abound to (names), that always having all sufficiency in everything, they may have an abundance for every good deed. As it is written, "He scattered abroad, He gave to the poor, His righteousness abides forever." Thank You, Father, You who supply seed to the sower and bread for food, will supply and multiply (names') seed for sowing and increase the harvest of their righteousness; You will enrich them in everything for all liberality. *(2 Corinthians 9:6-11a)*

Thank You, Father, that Jesus came that (names) might have life, and that they might have it more abundantly. *(John 10:10b KJV)*

PROSPERITY

The Lord be magnified, who delights in the prosperity of His servants. *(Psalm 35:27b)*

Father, I pray (names) will not walk in the counsel of the wicked, nor stand in the path of sinners, nor sit in the seat of scoffers. But that their delight be in the law of the Lord, and in Your law they meditate day and night. I pray (names) be like trees firmly planted by the streams of water, which yield their fruit in season, their leaves do not wither; and in whatever they do, they prosper. *(Psalm 1:1-3)*

I pray, Father, that this book of the law shall not depart from their mouths, but (names) shall meditate on it day and night, so that they may be careful to do according to all that is written in it; for then they will make their way prosperous, and then, they will deal wisely and have good success. *(Joshua 1:8 NAS/AMP)*

Father, I pray that (names) will listen to Your commandments, and will diligently obey You, observing carefully to do all Your commandments which You have commanded them, so that they may be blessed in all that they put their hands to, in the land which You've given to them, both in the city, and in the country, abounding in all prosperity. *(Deuteronomy 28:1-3,8,11 AMP/KJV/NAS)*

Father, I pray that in all respects, (names) may prosper and be in good health, even as their souls prosper. *(3 John 2)*

TITHING

I pray that (names) honor You with their capital and sufficiency from righteous labors, and with the first fruits of all their income, in order that their storage places may be filled with plenty, and their vats be overflowing with new wine. *(Proverbs 3:9,10 AMP)*

Father, I pray (names) will bring the whole tithe into the storehouse, so that there may be food in Your house. I pray that they will test You now in this matter to see if You will not open for them the windows of heaven, and pour out for (names) a blessing until there is no more need or room. Then You will rebuke the devourer for them, so that he may not destroy the fruits of the ground; nor will their vine in the field cast its fruit. And all will call (names) blessed, for they shall be a delightful land. *(Malachi 3:10-12 KJV/NAS)*

NEEDS AND PRIORITIES

Father, You did not spare Your own Son, Jesus, but delivered Him up for us all. How then will You not also with Him freely give (names) all things? *(Romans 8:32)*

Thank You, Father, You regard the prayer of the destitute, and will not despise their prayer. *(Psalm 102:17 KJV)*

Father, I pray that (names) will seek first Your kingdom and Your righteousness, in order that all these things may be added to them. *(Matthew 6:33)*

I pray they will be anxious for nothing, but in everything by prayer and supplication with thanksgiving, (names) will let their requests be made known to You. And Your peace, which surpasses all comprehension, shall guard their hearts and minds in Christ Jesus. *(Philippians 4:6,7)*

Father, I pray that (names) may fear You according to Your Word: for there is no want to them who fear You. The young lions do lack and suffer hunger, but they who seek You will not be in want of any good thing. *(Psalm 34:9,10)*

Thank You, Father, for supplying every need of (names) according to Your riches in glory in Christ Jesus. *(Philippians 4:19)*

For every good thing bestowed and every perfect gift is from above, coming down from You, Father of lights, with whom there is no variation, or shifting shadow. *(James 1:17)*

BLESSINGS

I bless You, Lord, for You daily load (names) with benefits. You are the God of their salvation. I bless You, Lord. *(Psalm 68:19 KJV)*

Father, Your blessing makes (names) rich, and You add no sorrow with it. *(Proverbs 10:22 KJV)*

Father, I pray that because (names) are generous, they will be blessed. *(Proverbs 22:9)*

I pray they be blessed to find wisdom, and gain understanding. For long life is in her right hand, and in her left hand are riches and honor. She is a tree of life to those who take hold of her, and happy are (names) who hold her fast. *(Proverbs 3:13,16,18)*

For You, Lord, give grace and glory; no good thing will You withhold from (names) because they walk uprightly. O Lord of hosts, how blessed they are because they trust in You. *(Psalm 84:11,12)*

I pray that (names) delight themselves in You, Lord, for You will give them the desires of their hearts. You know their days, and their inheritance will be forever. They will not be ashamed in the time of evil, and in the days of famine they will have abundance. *(Psalm 37:4,18,19)*

SATURDAY

Family

I. *Family - General*

Pray:

1. For unity and understanding.

2. For no resentment when sacrifice is required.

3. For sharing the vision of ministry; being active in it.

4. For sharing in prayer and devotions as family.

5. For each to operate in God-given gifts and talents.

6. For a hospitable home, open to others.

7. For all to be fervent in spirit, serving the Lord.

II. *Husband and wife*

Pray:

1. To meet provisions for family emotionally.

2. To be sensitive to family needs.

3. To communicate well with each family member.

4. To be a sympathetic listener to each family member.

5. For husband to lead family in devotions and prayer on regular basis.

6. To spend quality time with family—both leisure time and spiritual time.

7. To recognize they are a team, made to encourage and help one another with loyalty.

8. To complement and complete one another.

9. To discern each other's needs: emotional, physical, material and spiritual.

10. To have fruit of the Spirit in their lives.

11. To have fulfillment of own spiritual relationship and hear God's voice.

12. To have strength to overcome pressures and stress.

13. To resist living up to other people's expectations, released to be a unique person, and a unique couple.

14. For each to find individual niche in Kingdom of God.

III. *Children*

Pray:

1. That the children be trained in reverential fear of the Lord.

2. That the children show love, patience, understanding, loyalty towards family and ministry.

3. That the children choose righteous friends at school, home, work, and in their social lives.

4. For good relationships to prevail among the children in the family.

5. That the children be involved in parents' ministry at the level where God has called them to participate.

6. That there be no resentment or competition among family members.

7. That the children be obedient and righteous.

8. That the children be flexible, able to adapt to change, moving and culture.

9. That the children be free from expectations put on them by themselves or others that are not in line with God's will.

10. That the children be able to hear God's voice individually.

SATURDAY PRAYER

FAMILY - GENERAL

Father, in Jesus' name, I pray for (names). May they reign in life today through our Lord Jesus Christ, having received the abundance of grace and the gift of righteousness. For Your eyes are toward the righteous, and Your ears are open to their cry. *(Romans 5:17; Psalm 34:15)*

Thank You, Father, that because (names) have believed in the Lord Jesus, they and their household shall be saved. Thank You, that as for (names) and their house, they will serve the Lord. *(Acts 16:31; Joshua 24:15)*

I pray that (names) might be filled with the knowledge of Your will in all wisdom and spiritual understanding, in order that they might walk worthy of You, unto all pleasing, being fruitful in every good work, and increasing in the knowledge of God, that they might be strengthened with all might, according to Your glorious power, unto all patience and longsuffering with joyfulness. *(Colossians 1:9-11 KJV)*

Father, I pray that (names) will not be anxious, saying, "What shall we eat?" or "What shall we drink?" or "With what shall we clothe ourselves?" For all these things the Gentiles eagerly seek. For You know, Heavenly Father, that they need all these things. I pray they will seek first Your kingdom and Your righteousness, and all these things shall be added to them. I pray they will not be anxious for tomorrow, for tomorrow will care for itself. *(Matthew 6:31-34)*

Thank You, Father, that Your eye is on (names) because they fear You; they hope in Your lovingkindness, to deliver their souls from death, and to keep them alive in famine. *(Psalm 33:18,19)*

Father, by wisdom may (names') house be built, and by understanding may it be established. By knowledge may their rooms be filled with all precious and pleasant riches. The curse of the Lord is on the house of the wicked, but You bless the dwelling of (names), the righteous. *(Proverbs 24:3,4; 3:33)*

Because they fear You, Father, You will instruct (names) in the way they should choose, and their souls will abide in prosperity, and their descendants will inherit the land. Your secret counsel and sweet, satisfying companionship is for those who fear You, and You will make (names) to know Your covenant, and reveal to them its deep, inner meaning. Their eyes are continually toward You, for You will pluck their feet out of the net. All Your paths are lovingkindness and truth to them, because (names) keep Your covenant and Your testimonies. Redeem them, Father, out of all their troubles. *(Psalm 25:12-15,10,22 NAS/AMP)*

CHILDREN

Thank You, Father, that (names') children are a gift and a heritage from You, and the fruit of the womb is their reward from You. The children of their youth are like arrows in the hand of a warrior. How blessed they are to have their quiver full of them; they shall not be ashamed when they speak with their enemies in the gate. *(Psalm 127:3-5 NAS/KJV)*

You said, Father, that even the captives of the mighty man will be taken away, and the prey of the tyrant will be rescued. You will contend with the ones who contend with (names), and You will save their children. *(Isaiah 49:25)*

I pray, Father, they will train up their children in the way they should go, so that even when their children are old they will not depart from it. *(Proverbs 22:6)*

Father, thank You that all of (names') children will be taught by You, and the peace and well-being of their children will be great. *(Isaiah 54:13 NAS/KJV)*

I pray that (names') children be obedient to their parents in all things, for this is well-pleasing to You; that they honor their father and their mother, which is the first commandment with a promise, that it may be well with them; and that they may live long on the earth. *(Colossians 3:20; Ephesians 6:1-3)*

I ask, Father, that You give to (names') children the tongue of disciples, that they may know how to sustain the weary one with a word, and awaken their ear to listen as a disciple, and not be disobedient nor rebellious. For You will help them; therefore, they will not be ashamed, confounded, or turned backward. *(Isaiah 50:4,5,7 NAS/AMP)*

I pray that all may desire to know how to follow (names') example, because their children do not act in an undisciplined manner among others. *(2 Thessalonians 3:7)*

I pray that the fathers do not provoke their children to anger, but bring them up in the discipline and instruction of the Lord. I pray that the fathers not exasperate them, in order that they not lose heart. *(Ephesians 6:4; Colossians 3:21)*

Father, I pray that (names') children hearken and listen to You, that You may teach them the fear of the Lord. May their children keep their tongues from evil, and their lips from speaking deceit. May they depart from evil, and do good. May these children seek peace, and pursue it, in order that they may have life and length of days, and that they may see good. *(Psalm 34:11-14 NAS/KJV)*

And, Father, I pray (names') offspring shall be known among the nations, and their descendants among the peoples, that all who see them in their prosperity will recognize and acknowledge they are the people whom You have blessed. *(Isaiah 61:9 AMP)*

HUSBAND

Father, so that (names) may be above reproach, I pray that they provide for their own, especially for those of their own household, that they do not deny the faith, and be worse than an unbeliever. *(1 Timothy 5:7,8)*

Father, I pray that like as Christ was faithful as a Son over His house, so also will (names) be faithful over their house. *(Hebrews 3:6)*

I pray, Father, that they each may know how to possess their own vessels in sanctification and honor, and not in lustful passion, like the Gentiles, who do not know God. *(1 Thessalonians 4:4,5)*

I pray that the husband will live with his wife in an understanding way, as with a weaker vessel, since she is a woman, and grant her honor as a fellow-heir of the grace of life, so that their prayers be not hindered. *(1 Peter 3:7)*

WIFE

Thank You, Father, that You have made a suitable helper for (names). *(Genesis 2:18)*

I pray the heart of her husband trusts in her, and that he will have no lack of gain. I pray that she will do him good, and not evil, all the days of her life, and that he will be known in the gates when he sits among the elders of the land. *(Proverbs 31:11,12,23)*

I pray that strength and dignity are her clothing, and that she smiles at the future. I pray she opens her mouth in wisdom, and the teaching of kindness is on her tongue. I pray that she looks well to the ways of her household, and does not eat the bread of idleness. *(Proverbs 31:25-27)*

COUPLE

I pray their way of life be free from the love of money, being content with what they have, for You said You would never desert them, nor will You ever forsake them, because godliness with contentment is great gain. *(Hebrews 13:5; 1 Timothy 6:6 KJV)*

I pray they always give a soft, gentle answer to turn away wrath, because grievous, harsh words stir up anger. *(Proverbs 15:1 NAS/KJV)*

I pray that (names') love will be without hyprocrisy. I pray they will abhor what is evil and cling to what is good. I pray they will be devoted to one another in brotherly love; giving preference to one another in honor; not lagging behind in diligence; fervent in spirit; serving the Lord; rejoicing in hope; persevering in tribulation; devoted to prayer; contributing to the needs of the saints; practicing hospitality. *(Romans 12:9-13)*

FAMILY

And so, Father, as those who have been chosen of God, holy and beloved, I pray that (names) put on a heart of compassion, kindness, humility, gentleness and patience; bearing with one another, and forgiving each other, whoever has a complaint against anyone, just as You forgave them, so also will they. And beyond all these, that they put on love, which is the perfect bond of unity. And I pray they let the peace of Christ rule in their hearts, to which indeed they were called in one body, and be thankful. *(Colossians 3:12-15)*

As for You, Father, this is Your covenant or league with (names): Your Spirit who is upon them and who writes the law of God inwardly in their hearts, and Your words which You have put in their mouths, shall not depart out of their mouths, or out of the mouths of their children, or out of the mouths of their children's children from henceforth, and forever. *(Isaiah 59:21 AMP)*

DAILY PRAYERS

GLOSSARY

ANGELS - Spirit beings created to serve and minister to God (Hebrews 1:7).

ANOINTING - The presence, power and ministry of the Holy Spirit.

ASSIGNMENTS - A specified task or amount of work assigned or undertaken as if assigned by authority; trust and responsibility for completion of a task.

BODY OF CHRIST - All born-again believers in Jesus Christ; embodies all denominations who believe Jesus Christ is God.

CONFESSION - To speak forth acknowledgment of a belief; to disclose one's faults.

CURSE - To utter evil against one; to invoke evil upon; to call for mischief or injury to fall upon; to execrate; to injure; to subject to evil; to vex, harass or torment with great calamities.

DELIVERANCE - Setting a person or area free from demonic bondage.

DEMONS - Created spirit beings who were thrown out of heaven by God for rebelling against Him and declaring allegiance to Satan; evil spirits.

DIVINATION - The practice that seeks to foresee or foretell future events or discover hidden knowledge by the aid of supernatural powers.

HOLY OF HOLIES - The innermost section of the tabernacle and the temple of God. The High Priest went into the Holy of Holies only once a year, where he met with God and offered a blood sacrifice for the atonement of the people's sins.

INIQUITY - Gross injustice; wickedness.

INTERCESSION - Prayer petition or entreaty in favor of another. Through prayer this is an extension of Jesus' act of intercession when He died on the cross in man's behalf.

OCCULT - Literally "hidden." Hidden from the eyes of our understanding; invisible; secret; unknown; undiscovered; undetected.

PETITION - An earnest request of God.

PLEAD THE BLOOD OF JESUS - To remind oneself and Satan that he has no authority over the person for whom you are praying, because of the blood sacrifice made by Jesus Christ.

PRAISE (Godward) - To express a favorable judgment of God; to commend, speak, and attribute approval of God's character or actions (to Him).

PRAYING IN THE SPIRIT - Praying in a language unknown to one's own mind.

REPENTANCE - To turn away from sin and sinning and amend one's lifestyle to please God.

SATAN - The created cherub (angelic being) called Lucifer who was thrown out of heaven by God for rebelling against God and trying to steal His glory. The father of lies.

SIN - Anything in the creature which does not express, or is contrary to, the holy character of the Creator.

SORCERY - Magic; enchantment; witchcraft; divination by assistance or supposed assistance of evil spirits; the power of commanding evil spirits.

SPIRITUAL DISCERNMENT - The gift of the Holy Spirit given to Christians to distinguish between what is of God and what is evil.

STRONGHOLD - A fortified place. A place of security or survival; specifically dominated by a particular group or characteristic. One's thought life can have many strongholds.

TITHE - A tenth part of something paid as a voluntary contribution to God as an acknowledgment that all you have comes from and belongs to Him (Malachi 3:10).

WITCHCRAFT - The use of sorcery or magic; communication with the devil or with a familiar spirit; enchantment; unnatural power.

INDEX

RECOMMENDED READING LIST

Barton, Dave. America: To Pray or Not to Pray? Aledo TX: Wallbuilder Press, 1988.

Bernal, Dick. Storming Hell's Brazen Gates. San Jose CA: Jubilee Christian Center, 1988.

Bloesch, Donald G. The Struggle of Prayer. Colorado Springs CO: Helmer & Howard, 1988.

Boschman, LaMar. The Rebirth of Music. Bedford TX: Revival Press, 1980.

Bounds, E.M. Power through Prayer. Grand Rapids MI: Zondervan Publishing House, 1987.

————. The Best of E. M. Bounds on Prayer. Grand Rapids MI: Baker Book House.

Bryant, David. Concerts of Prayer. Rev. ed. Ventura, CA: Regal Books, 1988.

Chatham, R. D. Fasting: A Biblical-Historical Study. Bridge.

Cho, Paul Yonggi. Prayer: Key to Revival. Waco TX: Word Books, 1984.

Christenson, Evelyn. What Happens When Women Pray. Wheaton IL: Victor Books, 1975.

Dawson, John. Taking Our Cities for God. Lake Mary FL: Creation House, 1989.

Eastman, Dick. The Hour that Changes the World. Grand Rapids MI: Baker Book House, 1978.

————. Love On Its Knees. Tarrytown NY: Chosen Books, 1989.

————. No Easy Road. Grand Rapids MI: Baker Book House, 1978.

Eastman, Dick and Hayford, Jack. Living and Praying in Jesus' Name. Wheaton IL: Tyndale House, 1988.

Frangipane, Francis. Holiness, Truth And the Presence of God. Cedar Rapids IA: Advancing Church Publications, 1986.

————. House of the Lord.

————. The Three Battlegrounds.

Greenwald, Gary. Seductions Exposed. Santa Ana CA: Eagle's Nest Publications, 1988.

Grubb, Norman. Rees Howells, Intercessor, 3rd ed. Fort Washington PA: Christian Literature Crusade, 1983.

Gurnall, William. The Christian in Complete Armour. Lindale TX: Banner of Truth Trust, 1991.

Harper, Michael. Spiritual Warfare. Plainfield NJ: Logos International, 1970.

Harrison House. The Prayers That Avail Much.

Hayford, Jack W. Prayer Is Invading the Impossible. New York: Ballantine Books, 1983.

Jacobs, Cindy. Possessing the Gates of the Enemy. Tarrytown NY: Chosen Books, 1991.

Kinnaman, Gary. Overcoming the Dominion of Darkness. Tarrytown NY: Chosen Books, 1990.

Law, Terry. The Power of Praise and Worship. Tulsa OK: Victory House, Inc., 1985.

Lea, Larry. Could You Not Tarry One Hour? Lake Mary, FL: Creation House, 1987.

LeSourd, Leonard E. Touching the Heart of God. Tarrytown NY: Chosen Books, 1990.

Lindsay, Gordon. Prayer That Moves Mountains. Dallas TX: Christ For The Nations.

Marshall, Catherine. Adventures in Prayer. Revell.

Mathews, R. Arthur. Born for Battle. Robesonia PA: OMF Books, 1978.

Maxwell, John. The Pastor's Prayer Partners. Bonita CA: Injoy Ministries, 1989.

Moody, D. Prevailing Prayer. Moody Press.

Mueller, George. Answers to Prayer. Moody Press.

Murray, Andrew. With Christ in the School of Prayer. Grand Rapids MI: Zondervan, 1983 (first published in 1885).

————. The Believer's School of Prayer. Bethany

————. The Ministry of Intercessory Prayer. Bethany.

————. With Christ in the School of Prayer. Revell.

Peretti, Frank E. This Present Darkness. Westchester IL: Crossway Books, 1986.

Sandford, John and Paula. The Elijah Task. Tulsa OK: Victory House, Inc., 1986.

Shaw, Gwen. God's End-Time Battle-Plan. Jasper AR: Engeltal Press, 1984.

Sherman, Dean. Spiritual Warfare for Every Christian. Seattle WA: Frontline Communications, 1990.

Sherrer, Quin. How to Pray for Your Family and Friends. Ann Arbor MI: Servant Publications, 1990.

————. How to Pray for Your Children. Lynnwood WA: Aglow Publications, 1986.

Sherrer, Quin and Garlock, Ruthanne. A Woman's Guide to Spiritual Warfare. Ann Arbor MI: Servant Publications, 1991.

————. How to Forgive Your Children. Lynnwood WA: Aglow Publications, 1989.

————. The Spiritual Warrior's Prayer Guide. Ann Arbor MI: Servant Publications, 1992.

Shibley, David. A Force in the Earth. Lake Mary FL: Creation House, 1989.

Shields, Paula. Healing of the Soul. Bulverde TX: Intercessors International, 1991.

Sjoberg, Kjell. Winning the Prayer War. Chichester, England: New Wine Press, 1991.

Ten Boom, Corrie. Marching Orders for the End Battle. CLC.

Tippit, Sammy. The Prayer Factor. Chicago IL: Moody Press, 1988.

Towe, Joy. Praise Is. Irving TX: Triumphant Praise, 1979.

Wagner, C. Peter. How to Have a Prayer Ministry. Pasadena CA: Charles E. Fuller Institute, 1990.

————. Wrestling with Dark Angels. Eds. C. Peter Wagner and F. Douglas Pennoyer. Ventura CA: Regal Books, 1990.

————. Your Spiritual Gifts Can Help Your Church Grow. Ventura CA: Regal Books, 1979.

————. Engaging the Enemy. Ed. C. Peter Wagner. Ventura CA: Regal Books, 1991.

————. Warfare Prayer. Ventura CA: Regal Books, 1992.

————. Prayer Shield. Ventura CA: Regal Books, 1992.

Wallis, Arthur. God's Chosen Fast. Fort Washington PA: CLC, 1968.

White, Thomas B. The Believer's Guide to Spiritual Warfare. Ann Arbor MI: Servant Publications, 1990.

Willhite, B.J. Why Pray? Lake Mary FL: Creation House, 1988.

Wimber, John. Teach Us to Pray. Anaheim CA: Vineyard Ministries International, 1986.

NOTES